HOME GARDENER'S

Annuals

SPECIALIST GUIDE

The Complete Guide to Growing 37 Flowers in Your Backyard

CRE▲TIVE
HOMEOWNER®

CRE🏠TIVE
HOMEOWNER®

Originally published as *Smart Guide: Annuals* (978-1-58011-419-6) by Creative Homeowner.

This book is part of the Specialist Guide series. For other books in this series, visit *www.creativehomeowner.com*.

ISBN 978-1-58011-802-6

Library of Congress Cataloging-in-Publication Data

Title: Home gardener's annuals.
Other titles: Home gardener's specialist guide series.
Description: Mount Joy, PA : Creative Homeowner, [2018] | Series: Home
   gardener's specialist guide series | "Originally published as Smart guide:
   annuals (978-1-58011-419-6) by Creative Homeowner." | Includes index.
Identifiers: LCCN 2017037937 | ISBN 9781580118026 (pbk.)
Subjects: LCSH: Annuals (Plants) | Flower gardening.
Classification: LCC SB422 .S65 2018 | DDC 635.9/312--dc23
LC record available at https://lccn.loc.gov/2017037937

Printed in Singapore

Current Printing (last digit)
10 9 8 7 6 5 4 3 2 1

We are always looking for talented authors. To submit an idea, please send a brief inquiry to acquisitions@foxchapelpublishing.com.

Creative Homeowner®, *www.creativehomeowner.com*, is an imprint of New Design Originals Corporation and distributed exclusively in North America by Fox Chapel Publishing Company, Inc., 800-457-9112, 903 Square Street, Mount Joy, PA 17552, and in the United Kingdom by Grantham Book Service, Trent Road, Grantham, Lincolnshire, NG31 7XQ.

Contents

Metric Conversion

Length

1 inch	25.4 mm
1 foot	0.3048 m
1 yard	0.9144 m
1 mile	1.61 km

Area

1 square inch	645 mm^2
1 square foot	0.0929 m^2
1 square yard	0.8361 m^2
1 acre	4046.86 m^2
1 square mile	2.59 km^2

Volume

1 cubic inch	16.3870 cm^3
1 cubic foot	0.03 m^3
1 cubic yard	0.77 m^3

Common Lumber Equivalents

Sizes: Metric cross sections are so close to their U.S. sizes, as noted below, that for most purposes they may be considered equivalents.

Dimensional lumber	1 x 2	19 x 38 mm
	1 x 4	19 x 89 mm
	2 x 2	38 x 38 mm
	2 x 4	38 x 89 mm
	2 x 6	38 x 140 mm
	2 x 8	38 x 184 mm
	2 x 10	38 x 235 mm
	2 x 12	38 x 286 mm
Sheet sizes	4 x 8 ft.	1200 x 2400 mm
	4 x 10 ft.	1200 x 3000 mm
Sheet thicknesses	¼ in.	6 mm
	⅜ in.	9 mm
	½ in.	12 mm
	¾ in.	19 mm
Stud/joist spacing	16 in. o.c.	400 mm o.c.
	24 in. o.c.	600 mm o.c.

Capacity

1 fluid ounce	29.57 mL
1 pint	473.18 mL
1 quart	1.14 L
1 gallon	3.79 L

Weight

1 ounce	28.35g
1 pound	0.45kg

Temperature

Celsius = Fahrenheit – 32 x ⁵⁄₉

Fahrenheit = Celsius x 1.8 + 32

Safety First

All projects and procedures in this book have been reviewed for safety; still it is not possible to overstate the importance of working carefully. What follows are reminders for plant care and project safety. Always use common sense.

- ■ **Always** use caution, care, and good judgment when following the procedures in this book.

- ■ **Always** determine locations of underground utility lines before you dig, and then avoid them by a safe distance. Buried lines may be for gas, electricity, communications, or water. Contact local utility companies who will help you map their lines.

- ■ **Always** read and heed tool manufacturer instructions.

- ■ **Always** ensure that the electrical setup is safe; be sure that no circuit is overloaded and that all power tools and electrical outlets are properly grounded and protected by a ground-fault circuit interrupter (GCFI). Do not use power tools in wet locations.

- ■ **Always** wear eye protection when using chemicals, sawing wood, pruning trees and shrubs, using power tools, and striking metal onto metal or concrete.

- ■ **Always** consider nontoxic and least toxic methods of addressing unwanted plants, plant pests, and plant diseases before resorting to toxic methods. Follow package application and safety instructions carefully.

- ■ **Always** read labels on chemicals, solvents, and other products; provide ventilation; heed warnings.

- ■ **Always** wear a hard hat when working in situations with potential for injury from falling tree limbs.

- ■ **Always** wear appropriate gloves in situations in which your hands could be injured by rough surfaces, sharp edges, thorns, or poisonous plants.

- ■ **Always** protect yourself against ticks, which can carry Lyme disease. Wear light-colored, long-sleeved shirts and pants. Inspect yourself for ticks after every session in the garden.

- ■ **Always** wear a disposable face mask or a special filtering respirator when creating sawdust or working with toxic gardening substances.

- ■ **Always** keep your hands and other body parts away from the business end of blades, cutters, and bits.

- ■ **Always** obtain approval from local building officials before undertaking construction of permanent structures.

- ■ **Never** employ herbicides, pesticides, or toxic chemicals unless you have determined with certainty that they were developed for the specific problem you hope to remedy.

- ■ **Never** allow bystanders to approach work areas where they might by injured by workers or work-site hazards. Make sure all work sites are well marked.

- ■ **Never** work with power tools when you are tired, or under the influence of alcohol or drugs.

- ■ **Never** carry sharp or pointed tools, such as knives or saws, in your pocket.

Introduction

VERSATILE ANNUALS

Home Gardener's Annuals provides the information you need to include these remarkable plants in your landscape design. Annuals usually last one growing season, but they offer season-long color and texture to your garden. You can start them from seeds inside and then move the seedlings outdoors when the weather permits, or you can purchase seedlings and even started plants from home and garden centers. Use annuals in gardens and borders just as you would perennials and bulbs, and annuals are natural choices for window boxes. Also, containers of annuals allow you to change the look of your patio or deck as the season progresses.

Annuals come in a variety of colors, leaf and bloom shapes, and sizes. For these reasons, annuals are indispensable when combined with perennials and bulbs. Use perennials to form the backbone of your landscape; enlist annuals to provide swaths of color in your garden and to fill in bare spots. And you can experiment by choosing different annuals from year to year for your garden.

Home Gardener's Annuals will show you how to pick the best plants and provide the conditions to make your annuals thrive. There is also a section on drying flowers.

Benefits of annuals

What are annuals?

Annuals are wonderfully versatile plants. While some gardeners don't consider annuals "serious" garden plants, most think they are indispensable. A far greater variety of annuals is available in garden centers and seed catalogs than ever before—every year, you find a wider choice of colors, forms, cultivars, and even species.

USING ANNUALS

When used intelligently, annuals can serve a host of functions. No longer the poor relations in a flower garden, they are planted in beds and borders, either by themselves or mixed with perennials. They burst into lavish bloom early and continue to provide color as perennials come and go throughout the season. Annuals make excellent companions to spring bulbs, and their leaves and flowers eventually hide the yellowing bulb foliage. They can be used to fill gaps between shrubs and foundation plantings or can be grown around tree trunks, where their massed colors can brighten the shade.

Many annuals are classic container and window-box plants; they bring instant color to patios, decks, porches, and rooftops. They can intermingle with vegetables and herbs to dress up the food garden or soften the harsh look of a front sidewalk and extend a welcome to your visitors.

Annuals are a convenient and easy way to grow flowers in a whole spectrum of colors; you can find an annual to fit into any color scheme. Many make excellent cut flowers, providing armloads of blossoms for lavish and inexpensive bouquets. Some can be potted up in autumn and brought indoors to continue flowering well into winter.

WHAT IS AN ANNUAL?

To botanists, an annual is a plant that completes its entire life cycle in a single growing season. But to gardeners, the category may also include biennial plants that will bloom from seed in one season if given an early start indoors, as well as tender perennials that are killed by frost and thus treated as annuals in all but frost-free climates.

The annual palette contains all the colors of the rainbow. This garden (below, left) contrasts golden marguerites and perennial tansy with purple heliotrope and verbena.

Fill a corner with color by combining hanging baskets and pots of annuals. In the garden shown below right, sweet alyssum and lobelia freshen a warm mix of petunias and nasturtiums.

Durable annuals

Annuals growing near driveways, streets, and sidewalks are subjected to stress from dust, fumes, and traffic. Choose tough plants like those listed below for these difficult locations.

- Cosmos (*Cosmos* species)
- Sunflower (*Helianthus annuus*)
- Blackfoot daisy (*Leucanthemum paludosum*)
- Zonal geranium (*Pelargonium × hortorum*)
- Petunia (*Petunia × hybrida*)
- Rose moss (*Portulaca grandiflora*)
- Marigold (*Tagetes* species)

ANNUALS BY HARDINESS

Hardy Annuals
Grow best in cool weather; tolerate a reasonable degree of frost

- Bachelor's button (*Centaurea cyanus*)
- China pink (*Dianthus chinensis*)
- Flowering cabbage and kale (*Brassica oleracea*)
- Pansy (*Viola x wittrockiana*)
- Pot marigold (*Calendula officinalis*)
- Rocket larkspur (*Consolida ambigua*)
- Snapdragon (*Antirrhinum majus*)
- Sunflower (*Helianthus annuus*)
- Sweet alyssum (*Lobularia maritima*)

Rocket Larkspurs

Half-Hardy
Prefer cool weather but are damaged by repeated exposure to frost

- Blackfoot daisy, Melampodium (*Leucanthemum paludosum, Melampodium leucanthum*)
- Dahlberg daisy (*Thymophylla tenuiloba*)
- Dwarf morning-glory (*Convolvulus tricolor*)

Petunias

- Edging lobelia (*Lobelia erinus*)
- Flowering tobacco (*Nicotiana × sanderae*)
- Licorice plant (*Helichrysum petiolare*)
- Marguerite (*Argyranthemum frutescens*)
- Marigold (*Tagetes* species)
- Mealycup sage (*Salvia farinacea*)
- Petunia (*Petunia × hybrida*)
- Scarlet sage (*Salvia splendens*)
- Spider flower (*Cleome hassleriana*)
- Strawflower (*Helichrysum bracteatum*)
- Yellow sage (*Lantana camara*)

Tender
Need warm weather; can't tolerate any frost

- Cardina cimber, Cypress vine (*Ipomoea × mutifida, I. quamocit*)
- China aster (*Caistephus chinensis*)
- Cockscomb (*Ceosia argentea*)
- Coeus (*Soenostemon scutearioides*)
- Cosmos (*Cosmos bipinnatus, C. suphureus*)
- Dusty mier (*Senecio cineraria*)
- Fanfower (*Scaevoa aemua*)
- Fossfower (*Ageratum houstonianum*)
- Fuchsia (*Fuchsia* hybrids)
- Gobe amaranth (*Gomphrena gobosa*)
- Heiotrope (*Heiotropium arborescens*)

- Impatiens, New Guinea impatiens (*Impatiens* species)
- ove-ies-beeding, Joseph's coat (*Amaranthus* species)
- Madagascar periwinke (*Catharanthus roseus*)
- Mexican sunfower (*Tithonia rotundifoia*)
- Morning glory, moonfower (*Ipomoea* species)
- Nasturtium (*Tropaeoum* species)
- Nemesia (*Nemesia strumosa*)
- Rose moss (*Portuaca grandifora*)
- Sapphire flower (*Browallia speciosa*)
- Sweet potato vine (*Ipomoea batatas*)
- Wax begonia (*Begonia Semperflorens-Cultorum* hybrids)
- Wishbone flower (*Torenia fournieri*)
- Zinnia (*Zinnia* species)
- Zonal geranium, ivy geranium (*Pelargonium* species)

Zinnias

ANNUAL HARDINESS

Annuals are categorized as hardy, tender, or half-hardy according to their tolerance to cool temperatures.

Hardy annuals such as bachelor's button, calendula, and larkspur grow best in cool temperatures and can withstand some frost and freezing. They are often started from seeds sown directly in the garden. In Zones 7 and colder, gardeners can sow hardy annuals outdoors as soon as the soil can be worked in spring. Some annuals can even be sown the previous fall. In Zones 8 and warmer, gardeners more often sow hardy annuals in fall for flowers in winter or early spring.

Tender annuals such as impatiens, cockscomb, and zinnia are sensitive to cold. In most areas, they are started indoors and transplanted outdoors after the frost-free date, when the soil is warm. An indoor start is particularly important in areas with a short frost-free growing season.

A third category of plants—half-hardy annuals—is accepted by some horticulturists but not by others.

Half-hardy annuals are in between the other two types in terms of hardiness and include marguerite, lobelia, and petunia. Half-hardy plants like cool weather and tolerate a bit of light frost but are damaged by repeated exposure to frost and freezing. Gardeners in all but the warmest climates (Zones 8 to 11) start them early indoors and plant them out when frost danger is past.

STARTING PLANTS FROM SEEDS

Growing your own seedlings affords you a greater choice of plants and cultivars for your garden than purchasing plants from the local garden center. And seeds are much cheaper than plants sold by mail-order nurseries. You can sow seeds for hardy plants directly in the garden. But tender plants and slow-growing ones are often started indoors to produce plants that flower earlier than they would if sown outdoors.

Before you plant any seeds, be sure the containers and tools you plan to use are clean because seedlings are easy prey for disease-causing organisms. If you are reusing starting containers, scrub them out with a 10 percent bleach solution, and let them dry before filling them with soil.

Many people start seeds in a sterile soil mix or growing medium. A number of commercial seed-starting mixes are available, but you can make one from equal parts of peat moss, vermiculite, and perlite.

Add two parts of fully finished, good compost to this basic mixture if you want the potting soil to supply nutrients for the first few weeks. Although compost is not sterile, it usually contains enough beneficial microorganisms to combat injurious ones.

PLANTING SEEDS

Most seed packets carry instructions for planting depth and spacing. A general rule of thumb is to plant seeds at a depth that is two to three times their diameter. Tiny seeds (those of begonias or snapdragons, for example) can be mixed with sand to help separate them and make them easier to handle; sprinkle this mixture on top of the potting mix. Most tiny seeds need light to germinate, so it's important not to cover them after planting. When you mist the soil surface to water them, they'll work themselves into tiny niches that will keep them moist. Plant larger seeds in individual holes, or make furrows as you do in the outdoor garden.

Some gardeners cover their seeds with a thin layer of fine sphagnum moss to protect the seedlings from damping-off (a lethal fungal disease). Sphagnum moss has fungicidal properties. If you use it in your seed flats, make sure it stays moist at all times. When the moss dries out it becomes hard and stiff, and tender seedlings may have difficulty penetrating it. Although it was used to dress wounds during World War II because of its fungicidal properties, some people experience skin irritations if it gets into cuts or scratches; wear gloves when you work with it.

Temperature. The best temperature for germination varies from plant to plant. Generally speaking, tender (frost-sensitive) plants usually sprout best in warm temperatures of 70° to 75°F. Cool-season flowers germinate better in cooler temperatures around 60° to 65°F. Some plants need a period of freezing or cooling at temperatures of 35° to 40°F before they can germinate. Seed packets often supply this information.

Sow seeds that are large enough to easily handle one or two at a time into flats, cell packs, peat pots, or other containers of moist potting mix.

Carefully cover seeds that don't need light to germinate by sprinkling fine, loose, moist potting mix over them to the correct depth.

Light. Seedlings need plenty of light as soon as they break through the soil surface. Fluorescent fixtures are the best way to supply light for indoor seedlings. Their light is very even, and the plants don't need to be turned to grow straight. You can use special "grow light" tubes, full-spectrum daylight lamps, or a combination of warm white and cool white tubes. Set the lights on a timer so they're on for 16 hours a day. The tops of the seedlings should be no more than 3 or 4 inches below the lights for the first couple of weeks; later you can gradually raise the lights to 5 inches above the leaves. Start out with the seedling flats elevated on some sort of stand that can be gradually lowered as the plants grow taller. (A pile of books works nicely.) Or suspend the light fixture on chains that you can raise or lower as the plants grow.

Fluorescent lights provide a very even light to plants. For best results, use a timer to keep the light on the plants for 16 hours each day.

If you want to try growing seedlings without using artificial lighting, your best bet is a south-facing window covered with sheer curtains (to keep the heat from becoming too intense) or a bright, unshaded east or west window. Turn the flats every day to keep the stems growing straight.

Water. Seeds and young seedlings need to be watered carefully so that the seeds aren't washed out of the soil and the delicate new roots aren't disturbed. The best approach is to water from below, setting the flats or pots in lukewarm water in a sink or special watering tray. Watering from below allows you to evenly and thoroughly moisten the soil without dislodging seeds or tiny seedlings, as can happen with a stream of water from overhead. Set flats or pots in a container of water an inch or so deep until the soil surface feels moist, or use a specially made flat and wicking mat. This method gives you the most control over the amount of water your plants receive. Another technique is to mist the soil surface with a plant mister until the soil is thoroughly moistened. If you use this method, be sure to keep an eye on the soil.

Make sure your seedlings don't dry out; water stress can set back young plants permanently, so you will need to be attentive until the plants are well established. But don't overwater either. Constantly soggy soil encourages root rot and damping-off. Water your seedlings when the soil is somewhat dry—early enough so that leaves can dry by dark.

Feeding seedlings

Because the soilless mixes for seed-starting contain almost no nutrients, you'll have to supply some as soon as seedlings develop their first true leaves (the second set they form). But don't go overboard; overfertilizing seedlings can result in weak, floppy plants more prone to problems. Young seedlings can't handle full-strength fertilizer. Dilute liquid fertilizers to one-quarter the recommended strength (or if you use fish emulsion, half strength). Use the diluted fertilizer once a week for the first three or four weeks. After that, gradually work up to using a normal dilution.

If you've added compost to the seed-starting mix, you can probably wait to feed your seedlings until they are four or five weeks old. But check their color every day; at the first sign or yellowing or purpling, begin feeding once a week with a half-strength dilution of liquid fertilizer.

TRANSPLANTING PLANTS IN PEAT POTS

Seedlings in peat pots need special treatment at transplanting time; peat pots can be so rigid that roots have difficulty breaking through them. Set the pots in a water-filled tray for 30 minutes to an hour before transplanting. When you plant, tear through the sides of each pot, and place the seedling so that the pot rim is below the soil surface, left. You may need to tear off the top ½ inch or so; if the rim sticks out of the soil, it can dry and act as a wick, drawing moisture out of the soil and evaporating it into the air. On a sunny, breezy day this wicking action can cause serious water stress for young plants.

Harden off seedlings in a cold frame by opening the lid for a gradually increasing length of time over several days, finally leaving it open all night, middle.

Thin seedlings by snipping them off with sharp scissors instead of pulling them up to avoid disturbing nearby roots, right.

THINNING AND TRANSPLANTING SEEDLINGS

When the seedlings develop their first true leaves—the second set of leaves to grow but the first that have the plant's characteristic shape—it's time to thin. You can thin by pulling up unwanted seedlings individually, snipping off the stems at soil level with nail scissors, or carefully lifting and transplanting the young plants to other containers.

Spacing for seedlings in flats or pots depends on the size of their leaves, but 3 inches is considered a good average spacing distance. Crowding seedlings together increases root competition, encourages the spread of damping-off and other diseases, and causes plants to shade each other, which makes them spindly. To avoid problems, keep seedlings far enough apart so their leaves don't touch. When the leaves threaten to touch each other, the plants are probably big enough to go into individual pots or, if weather conditions are appropriate, outdoors into the garden. (See "Transplanting Outdoors," right.)

If you've grown seedlings in an unsegmented flat, cut the soil into blocks a few days before transplanting. The cut roots will heal before the plants are transplanted.

HARDENING OFF

Seedlings started indoors need to adjust gradually to the harsher environment outdoors. Leaves, like skin that's been indoors all winter, can easily get sunburned. Before you move your indoor seedlings out to the garden, harden them off. Over a two-week period, cut back on watering slightly while also increasing their exposure to colder temperatures. Begin by setting seedlings outdoors in a sheltered spot for an hour or two; then bring them back inside. Move them outside for a longer time each day, eventually leaving them out overnight. By the end of the second week the plants should be ready to move into the garden.

Another method that works well is to place the plants in a cold frame. Plants can be hardened off in a cold frame if you open the lid a bit farther each day, removing it entirely for the last two or three days.

TRANSPLANTING OUTDOORS

Transplanting to the garden is largely governed by weather conditions. The best time to transplant is on a cloudy, calm day, ideally in mid to late afternoon. Bright sun and wind can dry out transplants.

Dig the planting hole before you remove a plant from its pot or flat, even on a cloudy, humid day. This advance preparation should protect the roots from drying out. Planting holes must be big enough to comfortably accommodate all the roots and deep enough to allow the plant to sit at the same depth as it did in its growing container. If the garden soil is dry, pour some water into the hole before planting. Set the plant in the hole, and fill in around its roots with soil. Firm the soil gently; don't compact it. Then water the plant.

Protect your transplants from wind and bright light for the first few days. Floating row covers, made from lightweight spun polyester fabric, are convenient to use and effective for shading. Glass or plastic cloches, plastic gallon jugs with their bottoms cut out, and floating row covers all give wind protection.

SELF-SOWERS

Some annuals plant themselves. If you don't deadhead, or remove the faded flowers, their seeds drop on the ground and produce a new generation of plants the next year. If you like serendipity, let a few plants go to seed and allow the volunteer seedlings to grow where they will. If you want more control, transplant the volunteers in spring. And if you don't want to have volunteers, deadhead before plants have a chance to form seeds.

Many self-sown seedlings don't produce plants identical to the parents. The flowers are often smaller and the colors different. Petunias, for example, tend to revert to the magenta-purple color of the original species form of the plant. Such variation can wreak havoc with a carefully planned color scheme, but it can be fun to see what you get from one year to the next.

The following annuals are likely to self-sow in your garden:

- Bachelor's button (*Centaurea cyanus*)
- Candytuft, annual (*Iberis umbellata*)
- Cosmos (*Cosmos bipinnatus, C. sulphureus*)
- French marigold (*Tagetes patula*)
- Impatiens, bedding (*Impatiens walleriana*)
- Nasturtium (*Tropaeolum* species)
- Petunia (*Petunia* x *hybrida*)
- Poppy, annual (*Papaver* species)
- Pot marigold (*Calendula officinalis*)
- Rocket larkspur (*Consolida ambigua*)
- Rose moss (*Portulaca grandiflora*)
- Sapphire flower (*Browallia speciosa*)
- Snapdragon (*Antirrhinum majus*)
- Spider flower (*Cleome hassleriana*)
- Sweet alyssum (*Lobularia maritima*)
- Johnny-jump-up (*Viola tricolor*)

Marigold Volunteers   *Calendula Volunteers*

PLANTING SEEDLINGS

Most gardeners buy at least some annuals from local garden centers and nurseries. They're usually sold in plastic cell packs (sometimes called "six-packs"). It's important to know how to handle seedlings when you bring them home and how to transplant them from cell packs—whether into the garden or a container.

Resist the temptation to buy seedlings already in bloom, as are these celosias. Even though blooming plants provide an "instant" garden, younger seedlings not only transplant more easily but they are also healthier in the long run. Whenever possible, purchase seedlings that are still "green," or not yet in full bud or bloom.

PLANTING FROM A CELL PACK

When planting annuals in beds and borders, mark out the planting area and dig the holes, either one at a time or several at once. If the soil is dry, fill each hole with water and let it drain before setting in the plants. Push gently on the bottom of the cell to dislodge a plant, slide the plant out of its compartment without touching the stem, and set it in the ground. If the plant is at all rootbound, gently tease apart some of the roots, or encourage new root growth by cutting partway into the bottom of the root ball and pulling it apart a bit. Touching only the root ball and if necessary, the bottom leaves—not the stem—set the plant into the hole, firm the soil around it, and water well.

PLANTING A HANGING BASKET

Begin by filling the basket with potting soil to 2 inches below the rim. Set one or more plants in the center of the basket. Then plant several more around the edges, so they will cascade over the sides and disguise the pot.

For a fuller look, use a hanging basket made of wire. Line the inside of the basket with sheets of moistened sphagnum moss that you butt up against one another at their edges. Fill the basket one-third of the way with potting soil. Then insert some small plants around the sides, pulling aside or cutting through the moss so the plant tops are outside the basket, but their roots are planted in the soil. Add more soil mix to fill the basket two-thirds of the way, and add more plants. Then fill the basket the rest of the way, and plant the top as usual, with one plant in the center and three to five plants near the edge of the basket.

Baskets need to be watered daily in hot weather. To check whether a basket needs water without taking it down from its hanger, place your hand on the bottom and lift up so the pot rests on your hand. If it feels very light, the soil is too dry. When the pot has some weight to it, the soil is moist, and you don't have to water.

PLANTING A WINDOW BOX

Window boxes are a delightful addition to your home. They add instant charm to a country cottage and beautifully soften the severe facade of a city brownstone. Annuals are the plants of choice for window boxes, offering practically limitless combinations of color, form, and texture.

Plan your window boxes before you buy the plants. You'll want some taller and some shorter plants, plus some trailers. (See the list on page 14.) Choose colors that harmonize or contrast attractively with the colors of your home.

There are three ways to plant a window box: directly in the box, in a molded plastic liner that sits inside the box, or in individual pots that you place inside the box.

Plastic liners are the most convenient way to go, especially if you want to change the plants for different seasons. You simply pop the planted liner into the box. Liners are also easy to remove when the window box or the plants need maintenance.

If you plant directly in a wooden window box, be aware that constant contact with moist soil causes wood to deteriorate quickly. You can prolong its life by painting the inside of the box with polyurethane.

Planting in individual pots allows you to change plants during the season, but makes it harder to create a natural, gardeny sort of look. If you do keep the plants in pots, cover their tops with a layer of unmilled sphagnum moss.

No matter what kind of container you use, it's important to provide drainage. Purchase metal boxes with predrilled holes or drill holes in the bottom of wooden boxes or plastic liners. Use screening or row cover material to cover the holes.

Hanging basket plants

- Cascading petunia cultivars (*Petunia* × *hybrida*)
- Edging lobelia (*Lobelia erinus*)
- Fuchsia (*Fuchsia* hybrids)
- Impatiens (*Impatiens* hybrids)
- Ivy geranium (*Pelargonium peltatum*)
- Nasturtium, trailing cultivars (*Tropaeolum majus*)
- Rose moss (*Portulaca grandiflora*)
- Sapphire flower (*Browallia speciosa*)
- Variegated vinca (*Vinca major* 'Variegata')
- Wax begonia (*Begonia Semperflorens-Cultorum* hybrids)
- Wishbone flower (*Torenia fournieri*)

Potting soils

When planting in containers, it's best to use a light, porous potting mix. You can use a packaged preblended potting soil, as long as it contains a lightening agent such as perlite or vermiculite and is not 100 percent soil. Or you can mix 3 parts potting soil or topsoil with 2 parts crumbled compost or leaf mold, and 1 part perlite or vermiculite. If you prefer a soilless potting mix, buy one or make it by mixing equal parts of peat moss, perlite, and vermiculite.

CAREFUL TRANSPLANTING

1 Water first; then gently push the bottom of the cell pack to loosen the root ball. Rest the stem of the plant against your hand, but do not injure it by pressing on it.

2 Holding only the root ball, carefully lower the seedling into the planting hole. Fill in and press down gently to put the roots in contact with the soil. Water well.

Annuals for Window Boxes

- China aster *(Callistephus chinensis)*
- China pinks *(Dianthus chinensis)*
- Coleus *(Solenostemon scutellarioides)*
- Edging lobelia *(Lobelia erinus)*
- Flowering tobacco *(Nicotiana x sanderae)*
- Geranium *(Pelargonium* species)
- Globe amaranth *(Gomophrena globosa)*
- Heliotrope *(Heliotropium arborescens)*
- Impatiens *(Impatiens* hybrids)
- Madagascar periwinkle *(Catharanthus roseus)*
- Marguerite *(Argyranthemum frutescens)*
- Marigold *(Tagetes* species)
- Nasturtium *(Tropaeolum* species)
- Nemesia *(Nemesia strumosa)*
- Pansy *(Viola x wittrockiana)*
- Petunia *(Petunia x hybrida)*
- Plume-type celosia *(Celosia argentea)*
- Pot marigold *(Calendula officinalis)*
- Rose moss *(Portulaca grandiflora)*
- Salvia *(Salvia* species)
- Sapphire flower *(Browallia speciosa)*
- Snapdragon *(Antirrhinum majus)*
- Stock *(Matthiola incana)*
- Sweet alyssum *(Lobularia maritima)*
- Variegated vinca *(Vinca major* 'Variegata')
- Wax begonia *(Begonia* Semperflorens-Cultorum hybrids)
- Wishbone flower *(Torenia fournieri)*
- Yellow cosmos *(Cosmos sulphureus)*
- Zinnia *(Zinnia* species)

PLANTING A WINDOW BOX

1 Clean used boxes thoroughly with a brush and then a 10 percent bleach solution.

2 Plant the tallest plants to the rear, the shortest in the front, and midsize plants between.

3 Water well, and fill in any low spots with extra potting soil. Shade until plants are established.

4. Keep plants watered, deadheaded, and trimmed to promote season-long blooming.

A romantic window box (opposite) overflowing with cascading petunias softens a brick facade. Red and white flowering tobacco add height to the planting.

CARING FOR WINDOW BOXES

Because they contain such a small volume of soil, window boxes need frequent watering. You'll need to water at least once a day in hot weather. Aim to keep the soil evenly moist but not soggy or waterlogged.

You'll need to fertilize regularly, too. Water-soluble liquids, granular blends, and timed-release pellets are the easiest and most convenient fertilizers. Follow the package directions for quantities and timing. Fast-growing annuals will probably need fertilizing every two weeks or so, unless you use a timed-release fertilizer.

PLANTING LARGE CONTAINERS

When you plant a half-barrel or other large container with several kinds of plants, choose the plants carefully. Plan for a gradation of heights, like a miniature version of a garden bed or border, to create a sense of depth and a more interesting display.

For a full barrel, plan on buying three tall plants, four to six medium-height plants, and eight to twelve small or trailing edging plants. The barrel may look a bit sparse when you first plant it, but it will quickly fill in. If you stuff a container too full of young plants, either the larger ones will soon engulf the smaller ones, or all of them will languish after a month or so for lack of space. If you plant so densely that you have an instantly overflowing container, plan to fertilize frequently throughout the growing season.

Before planting, place the container where you want it. Unless you put it on wheels, it will be too heavy to move once it's planted. Make sure the drainage is adequate; drill holes in wooden containers and cover them with nylon screening. Fill the pot to within 3 inches of the rim.

PLANTING A LARGE CONTAINER

1 Plant the tallest plants (here, sunflowers) at the rear or in the center, depending on how the pot will be viewed.

2 Next, place the midsize plants (here, cannas) in front of the tallest ones or surrounding them.

3 Place the next largest plants (here, caladiums) either in front of or surounding the midsize ones.

4 Plant trailers (here, cascading petunias and sweet potato vines) at the edges of the pot to cascade over the sides.

By late summer, the sunflowers and cannas (planted above) will be in bloom, and the caladium, sweet potato vine, and petunias will be thriving.

Planning

How do I design a garden that will thrive?

The secret of successful gardening is to grow plants that are naturally suited to the garden's environment. That allows you to work with—rather than against—the plants' natural inclinations. When you understand the growing conditions in your garden-to-be, you can choose plants that will thrive in it. Always assess the characteristics of a garden site before rushing out to buy plants.

ASSESSING YOUR SITE

If you're starting a new bed or border, the first decision is where to place it. The best location for a flower garden is not necessarily the most obvious one. Consider the following factors when choosing a spot.

Light. A location that receives full sun—unobstructed sunlight for at least five or six hours a day—affords the broadest choice of plants. However, quite a few flowers prefer, or at least tolerate, light or dappled shade. Other plants, particularly spring bulbs, like plenty of sun when they are in bloom but can take some shade when they are dormant.

Wind. If your location is subject to strong prevailing winds, you will probably need to install a windbreak to protect your plants. The windbreak can be living—a row of evergreen shrubs—or it can be a wall or fence. Walls and fences used as windbreaks are most effective when made with an open construction that allows some air to pass through them. A solid wall can create damaging airflow patterns that may be as bad for plants as unobstructed winds.

Soil. The ideal soil for most plants is porous and crumbly. It contains plenty of organic matter and drains well while still retaining moisture. Light, sandy soils drain too quickly and do not hold moisture and nutrients long enough for roots to fully absorb them. Heavy clay soils pose the opposite problem— they are sticky and dense, difficult for plant roots to penetrate, and they drain so slowly that roots can become waterlogged and oxygen-starved. Few garden sites are initially blessed with ideal soil, but any soil can be improved.

    If you've never conducted a soil test or had one performed by a laboratory, it's best to have your soil analyzed for nutrient content and pH. A number of home soil-test kits are available, and some U. S. Department of Agriculture (USDA) Cooperative Extension offices provide a soil-testing service or can otherwise direct you to commercial labs. Directory assistance in your area should be able to help you locate a nearby Cooperative Extension or commercial lab. You can also find listings on the internet using the key words "soil testing."

    Choose plants whose needs match the conditions in your garden. For sunny areas, select plants that require full sun. Shaded areas call for plants that thrive in partial sun.

Pink lockets of bleeding heart are set off by greenish hellebores and other shade-tolerant plants.

TESTING YOUR SOIL

Plants depend on microorganisms to make many of the nutrients in soil available to them, so it's wise to test the soil for biological activity. A reliable and inexpensive test is now available for home gardeners. You can locate it by searching the internet for the words soil+life+test. Here, the blue test patch has turned green-brown, indicating high—but not excessive—biological activity.

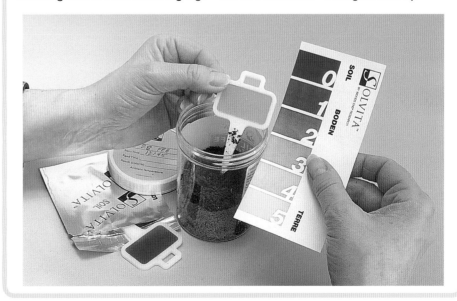

Where soil is poor or slow to drain, you can solve the problem by building raised beds and filling them with an improved soil mix.

The straight lines of a formal garden, with neatly edged beds bordering a brick path, draw the eye to the house with its filigree of vines.

Moisture. Soil moisture levels are largely determined by regional climate, but local factors can also be important. If your soil is dry, add compost, choose dry-loving plants, and mulch the beds. If your soil is generally moist, plants that prefer wet conditions, such as irises and astilbe, will do well. If your soil is almost continuously wet, build raised beds to improve drainage.

Temperature. Consider how hot your summers can be and how cold your winters are—your average maximum and minimum temperatures. You also need to know the usual dates of the last spring and first fall frosts. Think about whether snow lingers longer or melts away more quickly in your yard than in your neighbor's. Slow melting usually indicates the presence of a cold pocket. Cold pockets often form at the bottom of slopes because cold air tends to collect there. If you're new to gardening, or new to the area, your local Cooperative Extension office can give you information on the climate in your locality and tell you which hardiness zone you live in. Also consult the USDA Hardiness Zone Map and the Heat Zone Map on pages 92–93. (Note: When using these maps, be aware that conditions vary from year to year and that every garden has its own unique environments, called microclimates. The only way to really understand your property's microclimates is to observe them over a period of years.)

Ratings of both the degree of cold (hardiness zone) and amount of heat (heat tolerance zone) that plants can stand are approximate. You may find that conditions in your garden allow you to grow some plants not considered hardy in your area or, conversely, that some plants zoned to survive in your area just can't tolerate your temperatures. You will come to know the microclimates in your garden and learn which kinds of plants grow best for you.

After you've assessed the growing conditions on your property, you will know where the best spot for your garden is—wherever the best combination of conditions exists. But remember that you can have a successful garden almost anywhere by improving the growing conditions and by selecting plants known to grow and bloom in the conditions you have to offer.

Good garden design

- Start small and simple.

- Keep the plantings in scale with their site.

- Follow your instincts.

- Plan for a succession of blooms.

- Plan the flower garden to have some complementary flowers blooming when nearby trees and shrubs are flowering.

- Plant drifts of color, not single plants, and let the colors melt into one another.

- Have a gradation of heights, front to back, but let a few plants float in and out of their groups for a softer, more integrated look.

- Use a variety of plant forms and flower shapes: round or clustered flowers, flat daisylike flowers, trumpet-shaped flowers, talspires and spikes, branching forms.

- Be willing to change next year what you don't like this year.

- Remember to include a bench or chairs in your garden so you can sit and enjoy your flowers.

FITTING THE GARDEN INTO THE SETTING

Flower gardens should relate in terms of scale and style to the rest of the landscape and fit comfortably into their setting. Gardens that "work" on a property usually complement the architectural style of the house and its surroundings. For example, if the other elements on a property are formal, the garden should echo that feeling; if the house has a casual feel, an informal garden looks best. The garden should relate well to the other features on the property, too—the garage, sidewalks, fences, and walls. You'll need to think about the viewing angle or vantage point from which you want the garden to be most visible—inside the house, the yard, or the street. Because the most satisfactory gardens accommodate your lifestyle as much as they please your aesthetic sense, design your garden according to your needs—will you use it primarily as a place for reading and relaxation or entertaining and dining?

GARDEN SHAPES AND SIZES

Flower gardens come in various shapes and sizes. Edgings and dividers between different areas are usually long and narrow, while garden islands, foundation plantings, or complements to architectural features can take almost any size or shape.

Traditionally, all ornamental plantings (except for cottage gardens) were formally laid out and required armies of gardeners to tend them. But today, the old, rigidly formal styles have largely given way to looser, more free-flowing designs, and the grandiose scale has shrunk to proportions more in keeping with present-day lifestyles and smaller properties.

START SMALL

After determining location, size is the next factor to consider in laying out your garden. Gardeners always want to have more flowers than they can realistically handle. But nothing is sadder or more frustrating than finding yourself completely overwhelmed in June or July by spent plants with dead flowers still clinging to the stems, weeds overrunning the ornamentals, and blooming plants all but hidden in the wreckage.

It's best to start small. If this is your first garden, grow just a few different kinds of plants in a simple scheme of one or two colors. It's more effective to have several specimens of a few plants than one or two specimens of many different plants. Coordinating colors and blooming schedules is also easier when you're working with fewer kinds of plants. Repeating an uncomplicated plant grouping two or three times gives even a small garden a sense of continuity and a finished, well-planned look. Simple designs also make garden care simpler.

SITING FOR ACCESS

When laying out your garden, consider the practicalities of tending the plants while also thinking about aesthetic concerns such as viewing angles. Remember that you will need easy access to every plant in the garden in order to weed, fertilize, deadhead, and divide. Unless your garden is less than 2 feet wide, you'll need to be able to reach into it from both front and back in order to get to all plants. If you plan to install a border along a wall or hedge, allow for a little walkway along the back of the garden so that you can reach all the plants.

MAKING THE MOST OF LIMITED SPACE

If your available space is only a courtyard or small backyard, consider designing a garden as a series of multilevel raised beds. Instead of making one flat garden bed, you can make a raised bed that has two or three different levels and grow flowers on all the levels. This terracing creates an illusion of more space and allows you to grow more plants than you could in a single flat bed. Terracing is also a good solution to the problems posed by a steep hillside.

If you have no ground space for your garden and will be growing your flowers in containers on a patio or rooftop, it's still important to plan the layout carefully. You can group containers in various configurations and on different levels to create both height and depth, and even to serve as a screen. A well-planned container garden can look every bit as lush and colorful as an in-ground bed or border.

Gracefully curving beds and borders are ideal for an informal-style house. Add a bench to enjoy the profusion of color.

On a steep slope where space is at a premium, a series of terraces created by retaining walls makes more room for plants.

GARDEN STYLES

Choose your garden style based on the feeling of the setting and the architecture of your home. Formal gardens complement Georgian, Colonial, or sleek contemporary houses, while informal gardens suit ranch or salt-box homes.

FORMAL GARDENS

Formal gardens, like classical paintings, are built around controlled forms. Beds usually take the form of precise squares, rectangles, or triangles, with straight paths passing between them. They may be edged with low, clipped hedges of boxwood or other small-leaved evergreens, or they may have edgings of brick or stone.

Formal gardens exude an air of elegance and stability, thanks to symmetrical and balanced elements. Formal beds, and the plants in them, are often arranged along axes that draw the eye to a feature at their end—the house, perhaps, or a beautiful view, or maybe a sculpture. Some gardens have two axes, usually at right angles to one another. Planting beds are arranged along either side of the axis or axes, and plants and colors are often repeated from one bed to another to create both symmetry and unity. Paths in a formal garden are straight with sharply defined edges, and paved with materials such as brick, bluestone, flagstone, and concrete pavers.

The plants in formal gardens should be displayed in perfect or even an idealized form. Formal gardens are the place for evergreen topiaries—balls, cones, pyramids, or even animal shapes. This is the kind of garden where a fuchsia or lantana trained as a standard can take the place of a small tree as a vertical accent. (Standards are pruned to have a central stem that acts as a trunk.) At the very least, the plants in a formal garden should be neatly maintained—promptly deadheaded, meticulously weeded, and trimmed to keep them in their place.

Some annuals are inherently more formal looking than others. Larkspur, snapdragons, bachelor's buttons, fuschias, and heliotrope—though also at home in informal designs—possess an elegance and presence that is perfectly at home in formal gardens.

An understated color scheme usually works best in a formal garden. Blue and white flowers can be very serene, and a garden of all-white flowers looks crisp and fresh.

INFORMAL GARDENS

Informal gardens rely more on flowing curves than on straight lines; curved lines are natural and give a feeling of movement and dynamism. To design an informal garden, create your beds in graceful ovals or freeform shapes, and plant them so that low edging plants spill over and blur the edges.

Paths may lead off at angles or disappear around a corner to beckon you onward. In an informal garden, paths look best when they are paved with informal materials. Wood chips and pebbles are two good choices. Or you might prefer to use stepping-stones or even build a boardwalk.

You can use harmonious or contrasting colors in informal gardens. (See "Working with Color," page 24.) Or you might opt for a multicolored color scheme. Arrange the plants in fluid drifts of color and allow them to assume their natural forms. You will still need to stake some tall-stemmed flowers, but this is not the place for lollipop standards.

Formal gardens are neat and symmetrical, laid out in geometric shapes defined by careful edging. Most formal gardens depend on perennials to form the backbone architecture but make use of annuals, as demonstrated in the central circular bed here, to provide season-long color and interest as the perennials come in and out of bloom.

Plants in an informal garden can tumble together in happy abandon, leaning into their neighbors, clambering over fences or bushes, or trailing over the ground beneath the feet of taller neighbors.

TIPS FOR CUTTING FLOWERS

The best time to cut flowers is early in the morning before the dew has dried. Plants contain the most water then, so stems, leaves, and flowers are fresh and turgid. Early evening is the next best time. Although the blossoms contain less water after spending a day in the sunshine, the plants have been manufacturing food for themselves throughout daylight hours. Blossoms cut in the evening are well supplied with nutrients, which helps them hold their looks in the vase.

When you cut, take a pail of warm (110°F) water out to the garden with you and plunge the flower stems into it as you cut them. Be sure your cutting tools are sharp—dull tools can crush the capillaries in stems, making it difficult for the flowers to draw up water.

As a general rule, don't cut tightly closed buds or fully opened flowers. Most flowers last longest if cut when the buds are about half open and showing color. Some exceptions to this rule are asters, mums, marigolds, and zinnias, which should be cut when they're fully open. In all cases, take only flowers that are in perfect condition; those damaged by disease or insects probably won't last long. Cut the stem right above a bud, or at the point where two stems meet; that way, you'll encourage the plant to send out a new shoot.

When you get your flowers into the house, they'll benefit from having their stems recut under water. When flowers are out of water for even a few seconds, their stems seal off. Recutting the stems allows your delicate flowers to again draw up water.

COTTAGE GARDENS

The original cottage gardens were planted in front of modest homes in England and Europe. Early settlers brought them to North America. The colonists grew vegetables and herbs in their cottage gardens, as well as flowers for use in dyes, medicines, and seasonings. In the old days, a cottage garden was typically enclosed by a fence to exclude wandering animals.

Plants in cottage gardens are chosen for their individual attributes rather than their contribution to an overall design. This garden is the perfect place to grow "one of these and two of those." The old-fashioned flowers your grandmother grew—foxgloves and heliotrope, columbines, and asters—are perfect for a cottage garden. So are the cuttings and offshoots you receive from neighbors and friends. The serendipity of self-sowing plants is especially welcome here—let them come up where they will.

Gardeners today are creating cottage gardens in all sorts of regional vernacular styles. In the arid Southwest for example, a cottage garden might be full of native wildflowers and cacti, and enclosed with an ocotillo fence. In New England, the garden might contain stock,

Plants for a cottage garden

- Aster (*Aster* species)
- Bachelor's button (*Centaurea cyanus*)
- Balsam impatiens (*Impatiens balsamina*)
- Bellflower (*Campanula* species)
- Bleeding heart (*Dicentra spectabilis*)
- Columbine (*Aquilegia vulgaris*)
- Crocus (*Crocus* species)
- Crown imperial (*Fritillaria imperialis*)
- L Daffodil (*Narcissus* species)
- Flowering tobacco (*Nicotiana* species)
- Forget-me-not (*Myosotis* species)
- Foxglove (*Digitalis* species)
- Garden Phlox (*Phlox paniculata*)
- Garden pinks, sweet William (*Dianthus* species)
- Globe amaranth (*Gomphrena globosa*)
- Heliotrope (*Heliotropium arborescens*)
- Lavender (*Lavandula* species)
- Lily (*Lilium* species)
- Lily-of-the-valley (*Convallaria majalis*)
- Love-lies-bleeding, Joseph's coat (*Amaranthus caudatus*)
- Peony (*Paeonia* species)
- Pot marigold (*Calendula officinalis*)
- Poppy (*Papaver* species)
- Primrose (*Primula* species)
- Rocket Larkspur (*Consolida* cultivars)
- Salvia (*Salvia* species)
- Snapdragon (*Antirrhinum majus*)
- Spider flower (*Cleome hassleriana*)
- Squill (*Scilla* species)
- Sweet alyssum (*Lobularia maritima*)
- Tulip (*Tulipa* species)
- Johnny-jump-up (*Viola tricolor*)

Landscape designer Rosalind Creasy went back to tradition when she designed this front yard cottage garden instead of a lawn with shrubs and a few ornaments. Here, she mixes vegetables with a profusion of flowering plants.

nicotiania, and coneflowers behind a dry stone wall. What defines a cottage garden is the absence of rigidity and the presence of those plants the gardener loves best. Many people add informal decorative touches as well, such as a birdbath, bee skep, sundial, or small bench.

CUTTING GARDENS

One of the greatest rewards of flower gardening is having lots of blossoms to cut for bouquets and arrangements. If you enjoy bringing fresh flowers indoors, consider growing a cutting garden. These gardens differ from ornamental ones in that they are meant to be productive rather than decorative. Easy-to-access rows make maintenance and harvesting easy, and you can include all the colors and flower types you'll want for arrangements.

Most people put their cutting gardens along the border of their property or in an out-of-the-way corner, where they're out of sight. But if you're not concerned about appearance, put this garden close to the house so the upkeep will be easier. Vegetable gardeners often include a few rows of cutting flowers in the food garden where their color is a welcome sight and their pollen and nectar can feed beneficial insects. Herb gardeners sometimes mix flowers and herbs in the same plot.

Siting the cutting garden in full sun gives you the greatest plant selection. If the garden site gets less than five or six hours of sun, grow shade-tolerant flowers; you'll have a wider range of choices than you might imagine.

Flowers for a Cutting Garden

- Bachelor's button (*Centaurea* species)
- Blanket flower (*Gaillardia* species)
- Candytuft (*Iberis umbellata*)
- China aster (*Callistephus chinensis*)
- Cockscomb, plume flower (*Celosia argentea*)
- Flowering tobacco (*Nicotiana* species)
- Globe amaranth (*Gomphrena globosa*)
- Gloriosa daisy (*Rudbeckia hirta*)
- Pot marigold (*Calendula* species)
- Salvia (*Salvia* species)
- Snapdragon (*Antirrhinum majus*)
- Spider flower (*Cleome hassleriana*)
- Stock (*Matthiola* species)
- Verbena (*Verbena* species)
- Zinnia (*Zinnia* species)

PLANNING A CUTTING GARDEN

The following guidelines will help you plan a cutting garden:

- Put plants with similar cultural needs together.
- Lay out the garden by flower color, planting in blocks or rows of red, purple, yellow, and so forth.
- Choose flower colors that will go with your decorating scheme indoors.

- Grow a mix of plant forms to use in arrangements: tall, spiky flowers; rounded shapes; and small, airy "filler" blooms.
- Put the tallest plants at the back (ideally the north side), so they won't shade shorter plants. Place medium-size plants next and the shortest ones in front.
- Leave enough space between rows or blocks of plants to cut flowers, pull weeds, and perform other routine chores.
- In between the rows or beds, cover pathways with a good layer of mulch or plant grass to keep down weeds and make it easy to get in and cut flowers without getting your shoes dirty.
- If the garden includes perennials, try to plan for bloom in different seasons.
- Stagger succession plantings of the same annuals two weeks apart to provide flowers through the season.

MAKING GOOD USE OF CONTAINERS

Plants in pots dress up a window, provide a front-door welcome, and create the perfect setting for relaxing on a deck or city rooftop. Place large tubs of bright flowers next to the front door or set smaller pots with just one or two plants on all or some of the steps leading to the door.

Porches are another good place for containers of flowers if you place them where they'll get some light. Suspend hanging baskets at varying heights along the underside edge of the porch roof to create a pleasant effect. For a living privacy screen, or to shade the porch, let long trailers dangle from hanging baskets or train potted climbing plants on trellises.

Other good places for container plants include balconies, the paving around swimming pools, and the edges of driveways and paths. If you have several plants in small individual pots, group them on a fern stand or in a window box or tub to create a massed effect.

CONTAINER DESIGNS

Planning a container garden is just like planning a garden bed or border, but on a smaller scale. A well-planned design, whether it consists of many different containers of plants or several plants in a large tub or window box, still takes into account variation of plant heights and compatibility of forms, textures, and colors. The most successful color schemes for container gardens are generally those built on just a few colors. Pleasing polychromatic schemes can be more difficult to achieve in the confines of a container garden. But containers encourage experimentation, allowing you to try different color combinations that you can easily change the next year.

Caring for container-grown plants is different from caring for plants in the ground—the plants are much more dependent on you to supply water, nutrients, and the proper environment. When you cover the tops of pots with unmilled sphagnum or sheet moss to hide their rims, you are also helping them to conserve water. For other watering information, see "Watering Plants in Containers," page 33. Fertilizing information is on page 35.

Plants for a container garden

SUNNY LOCATIONS

- Annual candytuft (Iberis umbellata)
- Dwarf dahlia (Dahlia species)
- Edging lobelia (Lobelia erinus)
- Garden pinks (Dianthus species)
- Geranium (Pelargonium species)
- Marigold (Tagetes species)
- Nasturtium (Tropaeolum species)
- New Guinea Impatiens (Impatiens New Guinea Group)
- Pansy (Viola species)
- Rose moss (Portulaca grandiflora)
- Salvia (Salvia species)
- Spider flower (Cleome hassleriana)
- Sweet alyssum (Lobularia maritima)
- Verbena (Verbena species)
- Wax begonia (Begonia Semperflorens-Cultorum Hybrids)
- Zinnia (Zinnia species)

SHADY LOCATIONS

- Bedding impatiens (Impatiens species)
- Edging lobelia (Lobelia erinus)
- Flowering tobacco (Nicotiana species)
- Fuchsia (Fuchsia cultivars)
- Wax begonia, tuberous begonia (Begonia species)

HANGING BASKET

- Cascading petunia (Petunia x hybrida)
- Edging lobelia (Lobelia erinus)
- Fuchsia (Fuchsia cultivars)
- Ivy geranium (Pelargonium peltatum)
- Licorice plant (Helichrysum petiolaris)
- Nasturtium (Tropaeolum species)
- Sweet potato vines 'Blackie' or 'Margarita' (Ipomoea batatas)
- Trailing lantana (Lantana montevidensis)
- Tuberous begonia (B. Tuberhybrida)

Pots full of annuals along the front steps create a welcoming entry and can change from season to season, according to your taste and their blooming times.

WORKING WITH COLOR

Figuring out your color scheme can be the most challenging—and enjoyable—part of planning. Although there's no substitute for experience when combining garden colors, your own tastes should be your guide. This section offers basic guidelines for working with color. But don't be afraid to bend the rules. Let yourself play with color combinations on paper and experiment with them in your garden.

Consider the colors of elements in the landscape outside the garden too—trees, shrubs, walls, fences, and paving, as well as outbuildings and your house. The colors in your garden should work with these other background colors in order to look good in their site.

TYPES OF COLOR SCHEMES

Plan the color scheme in your garden to reflect your own taste. Do you tend to prefer harmonious, subtle combinations of colors, or do you like contrasts? What is the color scheme in your home? You may choose to repeat it in the garden, especially if you'll be growing flowers for cutting. Do you want a single color to dominate the garden all season, or would you rather have several colors working together?

On a color wheel, harmonious colors are located adjacent or close to one another, while contrasting colors are opposite or far apart.

Cool blues and violets create a feeling of calm and serenity—a respite from a busy world.

Contrasting colors are lively and active. Complementary colors, expressed here by orange geum and blue borage, are the strongest contrast of all.

Monochromatic color scheme

Contrasting color scheme

Polychromatic color scheme

Harmonious Color Schemes. Gardens planted in related, or analogous, colors are quite harmonious, but they can also be surprisingly dramatic. (Analogous colors are those that lie near each other on the artist's color wheel as illustrated opposite.) Consider a sunny yellow, yellow-orange, and orange bed of daylilies, cosmos, nasturtiums, Mexican sunflowers, and marigolds. Or try an autumn garden of mixed orange, bronze, red, and russet chrysanthemums, perhaps accented with a little purple. A beautifully soft mixture of related hues is blue, violet, red, and warm pink—colors found in flowers such as asters, bachelor's buttons, and petunias.

One way to achieve a harmonious mix of colors is to grow several cultivars of one type of flower—petunias, impatiens, or annual poppies, for example. The colors among cultivars may differ in intensity and in hue,

but they usually harmonize with one another. Or try different kinds of flowers in the same color, for example, calendula with golden cultivars of yarrow, cockscomb, and marigolds.

Complementary Color Schemes. Complementary colors, those that lie opposite one another on an artist's color wheel, create sharp contrasts. Orange and blue are complementary, as are yellow and purple, and red and green.

These color schemes can be unpleasantly jarring, or lively and jazzy. Pure complementary colors are the most jarring; for example, pure purple and clear yellow look harsh next to each other. But when the purple is deepened toward violet-blue and the yellow is soft and light, the combination is exquisite, as demonstrated by a pairing of Salvia 'Victoria' and 'Butterfly' Marguerite.

Contrasting Color Schemes. There are any number of ways to create contrast in the flower garden. The most obvious include pairing light and dark colors, pastels with intense hues, or complementary colors. Contrasting color schemes often look best when you use a paler version of one of the two colors.

Use the brighter color sparingly as an accent, and use the less-intense color over a larger area to balance the brighter color. For example, if you want to combine red salvia with blue lobelia, you'll get the best results by planting lots of lobelia among and surrounding the salvia. And you need only a few dark rose cosmos to add spark to a garden of pale pink flowers. To tone down contrasting colors, introduce neutral, or blender, tones as discussed below.

Monochromatic Color Schemes. Relying on one color to dominate the garden all season is probably the least complicated approach and the most successful for new gardeners. If you choose yellow, for instance, you might have daffodils and basket-of-gold in spring, yellow irises and potentillas in late spring and early summer, rudbeckia and yellow daylilies in summer, and buttery or gold dahlias and chrysanthemums in fall. Against the succession of yellow flowers that form the backbone of the garden, other colors can come and go. The other colors serve to accentuate—not compete with—the yellow flowers.

Monochromatic schemes generally work best in small gardens, where they give a sense of added space and openness. Those based on a light color can brighten a partially shaded garden. Single-color gardens need not be boring. You can vary flower sizes, shapes, and tones of color (pale, bright, or dark), as well as plant heights, shapes, and textures.

Polychromatic Color Schemes. Some gardeners like a polychromatic, or multicolored, scheme. Cottage gardens, with their cheerful riot of colors, are a good example of the polychromatic style. In a mixed-color garden, the variety of colors included depends entirely on the gardener's taste. Sometimes they work, and sometimes they don't. When designing, remember that strong colors modify one another when planted together. Blue flowers tend to cast a yellowish shadow on neighboring blossoms; red flowers look orangey when they're next to white

Blender Colors. A useful trick for integrating a garden and harmonizing colors that might otherwise be unsettling is to include blender colors. Groups of creamy white or pale yellow flowers make effective harmonizers for groups of stronger colors. Deep green foliage can be used to harmonize bright colors such as red and orange. Gray or silvery white foliage pulls together soft blues, lavenders, and pinks. And distance also blends colors that are otherwise quite contrasting when viewed close up.

This border relies on plants of varying shades of purple. Here white is a blender color that helps harmonize the different shades.

The cool colors used in this garden create the illusion of depth and space. Cool colors appear to recede (above).

Warm colors provide a stimulating and cheerful effect. Strong colors look best in sunny gardens; they tend to disappear in the shade (right).

WARMTH AND COOLNESS IN COLORS

Warm colors (pink, orange, yellow, and red) project themselves toward you, seeming to be closer than they are. But cool colors (blue, violet, and green) recede, appearing to be farther away. To create an illusion of depth and space in a small garden, try planting warm shades in the front and cool shades behind them.

Warm colors are also stimulating and active—even aggressive if they are strong—while cool colors are restful and quiet. For a peaceful, subtle effect, plant your garden in blues and purples. The cool colors will also create a feeling of distance. For a cheerful but not aggressive feeling, plant warm shades of apricot, salmon, and pink accented with touches of red and purple. Shades on the borderline between warm and cool— yellow-green, for instance, or rosy purple—may convey the cheerfulness of the warm colors and the calmness of the cool colors.

Finally, be aware that warm colors harmonize with other warm colors while cool colors harmonize with other cool shades. This is important in multicolor gardens because the warmth or coolness of a tint can make or break the color scheme. For example, if you're using pink with violet (which can be quite beautiful), choose a cool (bluish) shade of pink. On the other hand, a warm (orangish) shade of pink will be more effective with yellow or red.

USING COLOR EFFECTIVELY

Take care when selecting the color of the plants in your garden. Color is affected by location, sunlight, and other plants.

- Use simple colors that relate to the landscape and site.

- Plant in generous groups of color for the best effect; single plants here and there get lost in the design. Even flowers used for accent colors should be planted in groups of at least three.

- In all but the smallest gardens, plant in drifts instead of straight rows. Also plant a few flowers of each color over the boundary between adjoining drifts, so that the colors melt into each other.

- Avoid bicolored flowers in multicolored gardens (unless you really know what you're doing). Flowers in solid colors will usually produce a more sophisticated look, and they are far easier to work into a design.

- Dark colors are best seen close up. From a distance or in the shade, they tend to disappear.

- Pastels and white flowers can light up shady areas, where they gleam against the dark background. They are especially wonderful in gardens used at night or viewed as the sun goes down. At dusk, light-colored flowers take on a special glow.

- Strong, bright colors are especially effective in very sunny gardens. Pastels and dark colors are overpowered by strong sunlight, but hot colors are only subdued by it. Brilliantly colored flowers can also be quite striking against dark foliage, a point to keep in mind if you have foundation plantings of evergreens.

Working the soil

How do I maintain a healthy garden?

Digging new beds and borders is the hardest work in gardening, but it accomplishes several goals. First and foremost, digging loosens the soil so that plant roots can push through more easily. It also allows you to mix in ample quantities of organic matter to help keep the soil loose, fluffy, and easy to work. If a soil test shows you need lime or sulfur, you'll distribute it evenly if you mix it into the soil when you dig.

HOW TO TELL
WHEN SOIL IS WORKABLE

All gardeners are anxious to get into the garden in spring, but digging too early isn't good for the soil. In fact, you can break down soil structure and cause compaction if you dig while the ground is still half-frozen or wet. To tell whether your soil is ready to work, scoop up a handful and squeeze it into a ball inside your palm. Then open your fingers. If the soil ball sticks together when you poke it gently, the ground is still too wet to work (as shown in the photo at bottom). But if the ball crumbles easily when you poke it, you can start digging. If it's really powdery and dry, run a sprinkler until the top inch or two is moist. Wait a few hours before digging or tilling.

Test the moisture level in your soil before working it. Take a small handful and squeeze it in your palm. It should hold together but not show your fingerprints.

Tap the soil ball lightly with your finger. If it crumbles apart into irregularly sized pieces, it is just right, but if it compresses further, it is too wet to work.

ORGANIC MATTER

The importance of organic matter can't be overemphasized. It improves drainage in clay soils and increases the water-holding capacity of sandy ones. It also nourishes the beneficial soil organisms that make nutrients available to plants and helps to make the soil a healthy environment for roots.

Compost, partially decomposed leaves, and well-aged animal manures are all excellent sources of organic matter. Compost can also be called humus, a term for organic material in an advanced stage of decay. Decomposed organic-matter particles act like a combination of little magnets and little sponges—they create air spaces in the soil while also attracting and holding water and nutrient elements where plant roots can reach them.

It's easy to add organic matter while you're digging a new garden. If you need to improve the soil's structure, incorporate up to 4 inches per square foot of compost, peat moss, or leaf mold while you are digging. If you're blessed with great soil structure and are adding compost primarily for its nutrient-boosting properties, just mix it into the top few inches so that it's within reach of the oxygen-loving microorganisms that make its nutrients available to plants. (Similarly, greensand, rock phosphate, and other fertilizers only need to be mixed into the top several inches of the soil.) To add organic matter to existing gardens, keep the surface covered with a mulch of compost, shredded leaves, shredded bark, or another organic material.

HOW TO BUILD AN IN-GROUND BED

1 Remove the sod in the area where you are planning to make a garden bed by cutting through the root layer, in shovel- or spade-shaped blocks, skimming off the layer of roots and grass.

2 Remove the top foot of soil from a 2-foot-wide trench along the length of the bed. Place this soil on a tarp. When you are finished making the bed, you'll use it to fill the last trench you dig.

3 Loosen the subsoil at the bottom of the trench with a spading fork. If the soil has average to poor fertility, sprinkle a layer of amendments on the trench bottom before using the spading fork.

4 Fill the trench with soil that you dig from the next trench. Continue in this way—removing a foot of soil, using the fork to loosen the soil, and filling the trench—until the bed is completely formed.

porous, fine-textured planting area. But it is comparatively heavy work, and unless your soil is severely compacted and nutrient-poor, it's probably not necessary. Double digging involves removing the top layer of soil from the garden about a spade deep, loosening the subsoil below to another spade's depth with a garden fork, and enriching the topsoil with compost, manure, or another form of organic matter as you return it to the bed.

Power Tilling. A power tiller can be a labor-saving device for turning over new ground. But most power tillers won't dig more than 7 or 8 inches deep, so you'll still need to loosen the underlying soil with a garden fork. Stop tilling as soon as you have clods the size of a golf ball; you can level these with a rake before planting. Caution: grinding soil to a fine powder with a tiller destroys the vital air channels needed for good drainage. Also, using a power tiller routinely every spring to prepare annual beds can bring many weed seeds nearer the surface and encourage their germination.

MAINTAINING GOOD SOIL

Once the garden is established—especially if you're growing perennials—you'll be able to do less digging and rely more on the work of soil-improving organisms such as earthworms. If fed annually with topdressings of organic matter, soil organisms will maintain good soil structure and help ensure even distribution of applied fertilizers.

Established gardens benefit from the addition of a 1-inch layer of compost each year. When working compost and fertilizers into beds, scratch them in lightly around the plants' crowns (the area where roots and stems meet). Do not disturb the roots themselves. Also, be careful not to get chemical fertilizers on plant crowns because these concentrated materials can injure delicate plant tissues.

DIGGING

For most gardens, simple but thorough digging is all you need in the way of soil preparation. Remove any existing turf or weeds, as shown in the illustrations above. Using a tiller, spading fork, or shovel, loosen the soil to a depth of at least 12 inches—18 inches is even better. Then spread about 3 inches of compost or well-aged manure over the surface of the entire bed, and dig it into the top few inches. Rake the soil smooth before planting.

If you suspect drainage problems or have very heavy soil, you may need more elaborate soil preparation, called double digging. This produces a beautifully

HOW TO BUILD AN IN-GROUND BED

Build an in-ground bed in areas where a raised bed would be obtrusive or if summer droughts are common. Choose a site where the soil has good drainage, or add a layer of pea gravel to the bottom of the bed. The bed shown here is 4 x 8 feet.

1 After digging down to the correct depth, set stabilizing boards in place, and pound in four 12-inch-long 1x3 wooden stakes.

2 Continue removing soil from the bed until it is level throughout. To aid your eventual cleanup, place all the soil that you remove on a tarp.

3 Use a spading fork to aerate the bottom of the bed. Work from the middle to the edges of the area so that you don't step on soil you have already aerated.

4 Fill the bed with top-quality topsoil or compost, either bagged or home-made. Fill the area completely, but do not compress the medium.

5 Add rockpowders such as this azomite to the medium for added nutrition. If you're using homemade compost, amend it as necessary.

6 Fill the gap between the side boards and the surrounding soil; then use a shovel to level off the medium in the new bed.

WATCH YOUR STEP!

Once the soil is prepared, don't compact it; both roots and beneficial soil organisms need the oxygen it contains. Don't walk on planting areas or run a tiller over them. Provide paths to direct foot traffic, and make the growing beds small enough to reach into easily for maintenance chores.

A few strategically placed, flat stepping-stones will help you get into larger areas with minimal soil compaction.

MAINTAINING THE GARDEN

Garden maintenance will never be overwhelming if you keep up with it. Small weeds are easier to pull than big ones. A few pests are easier to eliminate than a full-blown infestation. Spending time in your garden on a regular basis enables you to spot and deal with problems before they get out of hand.

CONSERVING MOISTURE

Moisture needs vary from plant to plant, but unless you grow drought-tolerant plants or live in an extremely moist climate, you'll undoubtedly have to water your garden at least occasionally to supplement natural rainfall. With the threat of water shortages looming over us all occasionally, it's essential for gardeners to learn to use water as efficiently as possible and conserve it as they can.

There are several ways to conserve water and still give your plants the moisture they require. First, water only when necessary. The old rule of giving the garden an inch a week doesn't hold true for all plants in all conditions. A garden in heavy soil in a cool, cloudy location needs less, while a seashore garden in hot sun needs more. Soils high in organic matter retain moisture well; add compost to reduce watering needs. Instead of blindly following rules or setting the timer on an automatic watering system and leaving it at the same setting all summer, water your plants when they need it.

Conserve water by growing drought-tolerant plants if you live where summers are dry. Artemisias and other silver-leaved plants often tolerate dry conditions.

Plant annuals among perennials to keep the garden colorful all summer. This gardener is planting petunias to carry on the show when the irises finish.

Judging Water Needs. Check moisture levels frequently by poking a finger into the soil. When the ground feels dry more than an inch or two deep, it's time to water. Don't wait until your plants wilt or look limp; wilting indicates severe water stress. Some plants look a bit flaccid in mid afternoon on a hot, sunny day but perk up again later on, toward dusk. That doesn't necessarily mean they are suffering water stress. However, plants that look wilted in the morning or evening are in trouble. Water them immediately to avoid stunting and delayed development.

When plants need it, water deeply so that the moisture soaks far down into the soil. Deep watering increases drought tolerance by encouraging plants to send roots to lower levels where they'll be able to find more water during dry weather. In the long run, this strategy saves water because you'll need to irrigate less often. The

WATERING YOUR GARDEN

While watering with a hose or sprinkler was once the preferred method, it is rarely recommended now. For one thing, overhead watering is wasteful because the water must filter down through the canopy of plant leaves. Before it reaches the ground, a great deal of it is lost to evaporation, especially on a hot day. Another drawback to overhead watering is its potential to promote fungal diseases. Plants are especially vulnerable if you water late in the day and the foliage remains wet at night.

Watering from above does offer the advantages of cleansing the foliage and helping to cool plants in hot weather. If you must use a hose or sprinkler, do it in the morning or late afternoon, avoiding the hottest part of the day when evaporation is greatest. But if you water late in the afternoon, be sure a few hours of daylight are left so that plant leaves will be dry by dark. If that's impossible, get a bubbler attachment for your hose, and move the hose around to water all the plants at ground level.

plants will also be less dependent on you to supply all the moisture they need. On the other hand, if you water lightly and often—say, a quick sprinkling from the hose every day—the roots will stay near the soil surface where they will be more vulnerable to dry weather and hot sun.

Mulching is an easy way to conserve moisture. It reduces evaporation from the soil surface, while also increasing the levels of organic matter and helping to eliminate weeding chores. (See page 34 for information on mulching.)

WATERING EFFICIENTLY

To use the least amount of water and avoid diseases caused by improper watering techniques, apply the water directly to the soil. Soaker hoses and drip irrigation systems are two ways to water at ground level.

Soaker Hose. Soaker hoses are made of a porous fiber, such as canvas, or recycled rubber. They allow water to trickle out slowly. The hoses connect to one another. Use a regular hose to connect the soaker hoses to the outdoor faucet and turn on the faucet only partway. Lay the hoses through the garden early in the season. If the hoses' appearance bothers you, cover them with mulch.

Drip Irrigation. Most drip systems use lengths of narrow plastic tubing with small perforations along the sides. The tubing is connected with couplings to header lines. The headers connect to the regular hose and that connects to the water faucet. If you want the system to operate automatically, hook up a timer to it. Remember to change the timer settings according to the weather and the needs of the plants.

Depending on the complexity of your landscape, you may want to install a system with different zones. Zoned systems allow you to water one or more areas more frequently or longer than you water others. They are particularly useful for yards that contain a number of gardens with different moisture requirements.

Drip irrigation systems are sometimes installed under the soil surface, but more frequently, they lie on top of it. You can also find drip systems that are appropriate for container gardens.

You can assemble a drip irrigation system from a kit or buy the components individually. If your system will be complex, you can usually get a free design service and detailed installation instructions from the supplier. All drip systems are costly, and some require a fair amount of labor to install. But once in place, drip irrigation is effective and convenient, and does not detract from the garden's appearance.

Watering Plants in Containers. Plants growing in containers need to be watered much more frequently than plants growing in the ground. Because the volume of soil in a container is so much smaller than even a minuscule garden in the ground and because water evaporates through the sides, bottom, and surface of pots. This is particularly true of containers kept outside. In hot weather, especially on windy days, you will need to water potted plants in all but large tubs and barrels daily—small pots perhaps twice a day. The smaller the container, the faster it will dry out. Plastic pots don't allow moisture to evaporate as quickly as porous clay pots. Grouping potted plants also helps to keep them moist. But you'll still need to water container plants often. Check them every day—or twice a day—and water whenever the soil feels dry below the surface.

Soaker hoses allow water to trickle slowly out into the soil, minimizing waste from evaporation and efficiently delivering water right where plants can use it most—the root zone.

Mulch materials

MATERIAL	DEPTH
Bark chips	3 inches
Shredded bark	2 inches
Cocoa bean hulls	2 inches
Compost	1–3 inches
Hay or straw	4–6 inches in summer, 8–12 inches in winter
Shredded leaves	2–3 inches in summer, 6–8 inches in winter
Lawn clippings	1–2 inches
Wood chips	2–3 inches

Shredded bark

Cocoa hulls

Sawdust

Chipped leaves

Wood chips

Leaves

Straw

Lawn clippings

MULCHING

If communing with nature on your knees is not your idea of a good time, you can virtually eliminate the need to weed by mulching. Quite simply, mulching involves covering the soil surface between and around plants with a choice of organic or inorganic materials. All mulches help to conserve moisture and keep down weeds. A dark-color mulch can help warm the soil in early spring, while deep loose mulches keep the ground frozen in winter so perennial roots aren't damaged by alternate freezing and thawing action.

Organic mulches are the most attractive. They also have the virtue of being the most beneficial to the soil because they add nutrient-filled organic matter as they decompose. Most organic materials make good mulches, but there are some exceptions. Pine needles are so acidic that they are

Every time you remove a major part of the plant, such as flowers and fruits, or even the plant itself, you've removed nutrients that could have been returned to the soil. Make up for this by adding a general-purpose fertilizer.

WEEDING

If you choose not to mulch your garden, you will have to weed it. The best way to keep weeds at bay is simply to pull them regularly. Make it a point to weed the garden once a week or to pull a few weeds every day.

Make weeding as easy and efficient as you can by timing it well. Weeds are easiest to pull when they're small and when the soil is moist and loose. But don't weed immediately after irrigating or a rain because you'll compact the soil by pressing or stepping on it. Also, working around wet plants can spread disease organisms among them. Let the plants dry off and let the soil surface partially dry before you weed.

If you can't weed when the plants are small, at least get them out of the garden before they go to seed. If they drop their seeds, you'll have an even bigger weed problem in succeeding seasons. Don't put weeds that are going to seed on the compost pile. If you do, you'll spread the seeds through your garden with the compost and have a nice crop to deal with next year! Weeds that haven't gone to seed are fine for the compost heap.

good mulches for acid-lovers such as azaleas, but poor mulches for most of the plants you grow. Hay often adds as many weed seeds to the soil as it suppresses. And whole leaves can form water-repellant mats. However, if you shred them by running over them with a lawn mower, they make an excellent mulch for most ornamental plants.

When to Mulch. The best time to lay down a summer mulch is after the soil has thoroughly warmed in the spring and the plants are already several inches high. If you put down the mulch too early, it will actually keep the soil colder longer, delaying planting as well as retarding the growth of some tender plants. A 1- to 2-inch layer of fine-textured material is usually sufficient; coarser materials such as straw require more depth to provide good coverage. Mulch prevents light from reaching the soil between garden plants. The darkness prevents most weed seeds from germinating. Mulch also keeps the soil surface loose and crumbly because the sun can't bake it into a hard crust. Any weeds that do grow can be pulled out easily. All in all, a summer mulch is a tremendous work saver.

SOIL AMENDMENTS AND FERTILIZERS

All gardens require some kind of fertilization. How much and what kinds of fertilizer, and how frequently they need it depend on both the soil and the plants. As a general rule, if you remove a significant part of the plant, as you do when harvesting produce or cutting flowers, or if you're gardening in containers, the soil will need greater amounts of fertilizers more frequently. Vegetables and fruits usually require the highest levels of feeding, while herbs and shrubs (except roses) require the least. But there is wide variation within these categories.

CHOOSING AND USING FERTILIZERS

Gardeners often use the terms "fertilizer" and "soil amendment" interchangeably. It's true that both increase the fertility of the soil, but technically there is a difference between the two. A soil amendment is used primarily to improve soil (as by changing soil pH) or benefit microbial life, while a fertilizer is meant to provide plants with nutrients. Sometimes an amendment can act as a fertilizer and vice versa. For example, the compost you spread to improve the soil's drainage may also contribute important nutrients to your plants, and the fish emulsion you feed the spinach may help microorganisms break down a mulch.

The distinction between soil amendments and fertilizers is really only important when you are buying fertilizers. By law, soil amendments do not need to be labeled with their minimum analysis (the amount of nutrients guaranteed to be supplied), but fertilizers do. When you buy a bag of fishmeal, you'll find a series of numbers, such as 9-3-1, printed on the bag. These numbers mean that the product is guaranteed to contain at least 9 percent nitrogen, 3 percent phosphate (a form of phosphorus), and 1 percent potash (a

Every time you remove a major part of the plant, such as flowers and fruits, or even the plant itself, you've removed nutrients that could have been returned to the soil. Make up for this by adding a general-purpose fertilizer.

form of potassium). Fishmeal also contains a certain amount of calcium, but the law does not require manufacturers to label percentages of minor and trace nutrients. The table on page 37 lists the average nutrient content of many of the most common fertilizers and amendments, including both minor and trace nutrients. If you correlate the table with the results from your soil test, you'll be able to add the nutrients your plants need.

Nutrients are spoken of as "being available" or "being in reserve." This refers to the present form of the nutrient. For example, several commercial fertilizer blends contain about 4 percent phosphate in a form that plants can take up. However, they also contain close to the same quantity of phosphate that won't be available until soil microorganisms decompose and transform it. If you add this blend to a soil with low organic matter, you can't really count on getting more than the nitrogen and phosphate that is immediately available. However, if you also add compost or large quantities of organic mulches to boost the activity of soil microbes, more phosphate from that source will slowly become available over the next few years.

FERTILIZERS IN THE BAG

Numerous companies make blended fertilizers from natural ingredients. These fertilizers do not usually burn plant roots or injure soil life because they release their nutrients more slowly than most synthetic blends. (This also means they last longer.) However, such natural ingredients as Chilean nitrate can burn plants and harm soil organisms. When looking for a fertilizer, check the label. It should contain ingredients such as dried or composted animal manures, alfalfa meal, feather meal, soybean meal, rock phosphate, and kelp meal. The analysis of these fertilizers is lower than that of fertilizers made from synthetic chemicals; it may range from 2-1-2 to

For precision's sake, mix amendments and fertilizers such as this leaf mold, woodash, rockpowder, compost, and organic fertilizer blend before applying it to the soil.

8-5-5, often in the 5-3-4 range. If you compare them with the synthetic 10-10-10 sorts of fertilizers, it may seem as if you are paying far more per unit of nutrient. However, the organic fertilizers actually contain more than is indicated on the package. As microorganisms break down the materials, additional nutrients are released over time. Organic fertilizer blends also contain many valuable trace elements, which are missing from synthetic blends.

USING FERTILIZERS AND SOIL AMENDMENTS

In most cases, the best results come from fertilizing in the early spring. Exceptions to this rule are noted in the plant directories. Your soil test and the table will help you select appropriate fertilizers. In most cases, a soil that is deficient in one nutrient is deficient in others, too. And because you want to apply the proper proportion of one nutrient to another, the safest course is to start by adding a "complete" fertilizer that contains major, minor, and trace elements. Compost or one of the natural blends discussed opposite are your best bets. Follow suggested application rates on the label; avoid overfertilizing because it makes plants more prone to pests and diseases.

Sometimes a plant is more deficient in one nutrient than others. If the lab that tested your soil recommended natural fertilizers, all you have to do is follow its directions. But if you want to create your own mixes, you'll need to do some math. Strive for a proportion of two to four times as much nitrogen to phosphate, and one to two times as much potash as nitrogen. However, most perennial fruiting and flowering crops require slightly less nitrogen relative to phosphate and potash; and perennial herbs require even less nitrogen.

NET WEIGHT 40

QUIK GREEN 5-10-5

GUARANTEED ANALYSIS

Total Nitrogen (N) 5%
Available Phosphate (P₂O₅) 10%
Soluble Potash (K₂O) 5%

Fertilizers derived from chemical treatment give larger amounts of immediately available nutrients but can injure delicate roots and beneficial soil organisms.

NUTRIENT CONTRIBUTIONS OF COMMON SOIL AMENDMENTS AND FERTILIZERS

Soil amendments and fertilizers derived from natural sources often contain much more than simply mineral nutrients. The table below lists some of their other benefits as well as giving application rates.

Material	Primary Benefits	Analysis (N-P-K, plus minor & trace nutrients)	Average Application Rate per 1,000 sq. ft. when Soils Test:			Notes
			Low	Moderate	Adequate	
Alfalfa meal	Organic, matter, nitrogen	5-1-2	50 lbs.	35 lbs.	25 lbs.	Contains a natural growth stimulant plus trace elements
Aragonite	Calcium	96% calcium carbonate	100 lbs.	50 lbs.	25 lbs.	Can replace limestone
Calcitic lime		65-80% calcium carbonate 3-15% magnesium carbonate	Use soil test; quantity depends on soil type as well as pH			Use in soils with adequate magnesium and low calcium
Colloidal phosphate	Phosphate	0-2-2	60 lbs.	25 lbs.	10 lbs.	Adds to soil reserves as well as available quantity
Compost	Organic matter, soil life	0.5-0.5-0.5 to 3-3-3	200 lbs.	100 lbs.	10 lbs.	Adds balanced nutrients & the soil life to make them available
Dolomitic lime	Calcium magnesium	51% calcium carbonate 40% magnesium carbonate	Use soil test; quantity depends on soil type as well as pH			Use in soils with low magnesium low calcium
Epsom Salts	Magnesium, sulfur	10% magnesium, 13% sulfur	5 lbs.	3 lbs.	1 lbs.	Use when magnesium is so low that other sources won't work
Fish emulsion	Nitrogen	4-1-1; 5% sulfur	2 oz.	1 oz.	1 oz.	Can be used as a foliar feed too, mix 50/50 with liquid seaweed, and dilute to half the recommended strength
Granite meal	Potash, trace elements	4% total potash; 67% silicas, 19 trace elements	100 lbs.	50 lbs.	25 lbs.	Rock powders add to long-term soil fertility and health
Greensand	Potash, trace elements	7% potash, 32 trace minerals	100 lbs.	50 lbs.	25 lbs.	Excellent potash source
Kelp meal	Potash, trace elements	1.5-0.5-2.5	20 lbs.	10 lbs.	5 lbs.	Best for spot applications where extra potash is needed
Rock phosphate	Phosphate	0-3-3; 32% calcium, 11 trace elements	60 lbs.	25 lbs.	10 lbs.	Apply when you start the garden and every four years once soil phosphate levels are adequate
Soybean meal	Mitrogen	7-0.5-2.3	50 lbs.	25 lbs.	10 lbs.	Excellent soil amendment during the second half of the season
Sul-Po-Mag	Sulfur, potash, magnesium	0-0-22; 11% magnesium 22% sulfur	10 lbs.	7 lbs.	5 lbs.	Use only if magnesium levels are low & never with dolomitic lime
Worm castings	Organic Matter	0.5-0.5-0.3	n/a	n/a	n/a	Use in potting soils and for spot fertilizing

Minimize disease problems by choosing resistant cultivars whenever possible. Zinnias are prone to powdery mildew, especially late in the season. However, 'Pulcino' and the Star hybrids are among the cultivars bred to be resistant to this disease.

Keeping plants healthy

- Build your soil every year with compost or other organic matter to provide the best possible growing medium for plants.

- Be sure an adequate supply of nutrients is available for plants, but don't overfeed them. Overfertilizing stimulates fast, weak growth that is extremely susceptible to pest damage.

- Water plants when they need it, but don't overwater. Plants stressed by too much or too little moisture will be weakened.

CONTROLLING PESTS AND DISEASES

The gardener's most important lines of defense against garden thugs are good garden practices: taking preventive measures, practicing good sanitation, maintaining the plants well, and intervening at the first sign of any problem.

PREVENTIVE MEASURES

Although you can't keep pests and diseases from invading your garden, you can do several things to make your garden less inviting to them. First and foremost, practice good sanitation. Simply keep the garden clean. Keep up with the weeding and pick up dead leaves, flowers, and other trash that falls to the ground. Plant debris provides excellent hiding places for pests to overwinter and lay their eggs, as well as sites for disease organisms to take hold.

You can spread disease organisms from one plant to another just by working in the garden, so be careful. Don't work in the garden when plants are wet; your hands, tools, or clothes could transfer harmful organisms that are in the water on the leaves. Don't smoke in the garden; if you smoke at all, wash your hands before working around your plants. (Tobacco carries plant viruses.) Keep infested plant materials out of the compost pile.

Avoid crowding plants together when planting. Plants need sufficient room to develop properly if they are to remain vigorous. Good air circulation helps to prevent fungal diseases and some pests that thrive in high-humidity conditions. Mixed plantings also have fewer problems than entire beds or large blocks of a single type of plant because they confuse insects that rely on odor or visual cues to find their hosts.

If your plants are attacked by the same pest and disease problems year after year, seek out plants that don't tend to get those problems, or plant varieties resistant to them. For example, if your zinnias always seem to get powdery mildew, look for varieties bred for resistance to it, such as 'Pulcino' or the Star hybrids. Growing pest- and disease-susceptible plants in a different part of the garden each year deprives pest and disease organisms of appropriate hosts. This simple straegy can prevent them from building high populations.

MONITOR THE GARDEN

Keep a close watch on all your plants throughout the growing season, and take action whenever you notice the first signs of pests or a disease. Examine several representative plants of each type carefully, checking the leaf axils, undersides of leaves, growing tips, and flower buds for diseases or pest insects and their eggs. Remove diseased or severely pest-infested parts of plants as soon

Learn to identify insect eggs—these will eventually hatch into larvae of one of the most useful insects in the garden, ladybugs.

as you see them. To avoid spreading the problem, place the debris in a plastic bag and put it in the trash. These problems are easiest to solve in their early stages, before the pest population assumes major proportions or the disease spreads to several plants.

PEST CONTROL

The safest pest controls include traps, biological controls, and natural and plant-based materials that quickly break down into noninjurious substances after they are applied.

Lace wing adults, above, and larvae, right, feed on aphids, mites, and other small, soft-bodied pests. Adults require nectar and pollen in order to reproduce.

Sticky yellow traps suspended among plants are effective against aphids and especially whiteflies. These insects are attracted by the bright yellow color of the traps and stick to the adhesive coating. When the trap is covered with bugs, wipe it off and recoat it with commercially available Tanglefoot or just discard it.

Blue and white sticky traps are also available. Thrips are attracted to blue traps, while tarnished plant bugs, or Lygus bugs, favor white ones. Again, the traps should be cleaned off and recoated or discarded when they lose their stickiness or run out of uncovered area.

Insecticidal soap is effective against aphids, whiteflies, flea beetles, and other small pests; it simply clogs their breathing holes. Plant-based insecticides include pyrethrum, neem, ryania, and sabadilla. These materials kill fairly selectively. (See the label.) However, because they can kill some benign or beneficial insects along with pests, use them with care. Rotenone, a botanical pesticide which is often recommended, kills so many insect species that it's best to use it only as the very last resort.

Biological controls are even more specific than botanical insecticides. Bacillus thuringiensis var. kurstaki (a bacterium sold as BTK or Dipel) is effective against all caterpillars. Diatomaceous earth, ground diatom skeletons, controls soft-bodied pests. If you use diatomaceous earth, buy a brand meant for horticultural use rather than the type sold for use in swimming pool filters.

Most organic insecticides and controls must be reapplied after it rains, but the extra effort seems a small price to pay for the peace of mind they afford.

Familiarize yourself with the beneficial insects in your garden—the helpful predators and parasitoids of the pests. Learn to recognize ladybugs, praying mantids, green lacewings, and other allies. If you spot them, leave them alone and consider yourself lucky. You can also purchase beneficial insects by mail to release into your garden.

FIGHTING DISEASE

Early intervention is the best weapon against plant diseases. If you notice disease symptoms, immediately remove the affected part of the plant. If more symptoms develop, pull up the entire plant and put it in the trash. Never put diseased plant material on the compost pile; even a hot pile doesn't get hot enough to destroy all types of pathogens. Sulfur and copper sprays can help control fungus and some bacterial problems before they take hold.

Read the labels on all fungicides before using them; some injure plants at certain temperatures. Also make certain that the product works on the disease you're trying to control and is safe for the plant you're treating.

JAPANESE BEETLES

If Japanese beetles are a perennial problem for you and you live in Zones 6-10, sprinkle milky spore disease on the soil around affected plants. This disease kills the grubs that winter over in your lawn. In colder areas, apply predatory nematodes to the soil in the spring. (Both milky spore disease and beneficial nematodes are sold under several trade names and are available at most garden centers.) Pheromone traps can be helpful in controlling adult Japanese beetles, but they can actually lure more beetles to your garden if you place them too close to the area.

Potting mix ingredients for annuals include soil, lightening agents such as peat moss, perlite and vermiculite, and organic or synthetic fertilizers to supply nutrients.

CARING FOR ANNUALS

Annuals are easy to grow and care for as long as you pay attention to the basics. Make certain that the soil is well prepared in the beginning of the season and that the environment—light, temperature, and soil qualities—suits the plants you're growing. Aside from these considerations, your major tasks will be to provide these fast-growing plants with plenty of water and fertilizer. Depending on the plant, faded flowers must also be removed and foliage cut back after the first blooms are spent.

WATERING

Whether growing in the ground or in containers, newly transplanted annuals need constant, even moisture for the first couple of weeks while they establish themselves. Thereafter, water according to the plants' needs. Some, such as rose moss, prefer drier conditions than do moisture lovers such as floss flower. (See "Favorites," pages 52–91, for moisture needs.)

Soaker hoses are a convenient and efficient way to water annuals in beds and borders—they allow water to trickle out slowly so it can be easily absorbed into the soil. For hanging baskets and other containers, a hose with a watering wand lets you water without a lot of stretching or bending.

FERTILIZING ANNUALS

Annuals need regular fertilization to fuel their rapid growth. Remember, annuals go through their entire life cycle in a single growing season. Healthy soil that contains plenty of organic matter will sustain the growth of many annuals, but sometimes your plants will need an extra nutrient boost.

If you choose organic fertilizers, bear in mind that many of these take time to break down in the soil and release their nutrients. You'll have to apply granular and powdered formulas ahead of time. Fortunately, there are two easy organic options that provide instant nutrition to plants: liquid seaweed and fish emulsion. Either is good for annuals; but using both provides complete nutrition. Dilute according to label directions before applying with a watering can or, for fast results, spray a half-strength dilution on leaves in low-light conditions (before sunrise or on a cloudy day).

For flowering annuals, an all-purpose fertilizer, such as a 5-10-5 or a 15-30-15 (or, if organic, 3-4-3 or 4-5-4) formula works best. Foliage plants will thrive with a fertilizer high in nitrogen (indicated by the first number in the series). Use a granular, timed-release, or compost-based fertilizer for annuals in beds and borders; water-soluble fertilizers are best for container plants. Follow the package directions for application rates and frequency.

DRIP SYSTEM

Setting up drip systems with spaghetti tubes and individual emitters is easy if you follow the manufacturer's directions. These systems can be arranged to water pots as well as in-ground plants in the same area, as long as the plants' water needs are similar.

When deadheading, clip off spent flower stems back to the next set of leaves to avoid leaving bare stems.

DEADHEADING

An annual plant's mission is to bloom, produce seeds, and then die. To keep plants blooming, prevent them from setting seeds. Deadheading—removing faded flowers before seeds develop—frustrates a plant's attempt to complete its life cycle and encourages it to keep producing flowers.

When deadheading, don't just snip off the flower and leave the bare stem. Instead, cut off the stem right above the next lower set of leaves. One exception to this rule is flowering tobacco. If you cut off a faded flower just under its base, new flowers will form on the stem right below the site of the old blossom.

Some plants with lots of small flowers, particularly lobelia and sweet alyssum, are hard to deadhead. To renew these plants if flowering slows, shear back the plants rather than snipping stems. (See "Favorites," pages 52–91.)

When Not to Deadhead. Many popular annuals self-sow if you let them. If you want particular plants to self-sow, or if you want to collect and save seeds for next year's garden, don't deadhead all the plants. Choose the healthiest, best-looking specimens of the types you want to save, and let them form seeds in the latter part of their seasons.

Biennials that self-sow come up the same year and overwinter as small plants. Self-sown seedlings of true annuals won't appear until the following spring. To prevent overcrowding, you usually have to thin them or transplant to new spots. To avoid weeding them out when they first appear, pay attention to the appearance of both their seed leaves and first true leaves.

Deadheading is the key to keeping annuals in bloom all season. Snipping off spent blossoms prevents plants from setting seeds, so they produce more flowers.

END-OF-SEASON CARE

As the outdoor growing season winds down in fall, pull up all your spent annuals and toss them on the compost pile. (Throw out all China asters and any diseased plants.) If you plan to sow seeds of hardy annuals in fall for winter or spring bloom, prepare their planting areas. Spread a layer of compost and, if using them, organic fertilizers, and incoporate into the soil. Sow hardy annuals at the correct time for your area. (If you are unsure about when to plant, ask a gardening friend or call your local Cooperative Extension Service for advice.)

Remove annuals from window boxes and other containers, and dump the potting soil in your garden (as long as the plants weren't afflicted with a disease). Scrub out the containers, and store them for the winter.

COLLECTING AND SAVING SEEDS

One of the great pleasures of growing annuals is the ease with which you can save their seeds. It's fun to save seeds from your favorite plants. You can sow them the following year, share them with friends, or give them to the birds. If you grow heirloom varieties and save their seeds, you'll help to keep these treasured plants from disappearing forever. You can even try your hand at plant breeding after a few years of practice, selecting for qualities you most want in your plants, and cross-pollinating to create your own hybrids.

If you want the seeds you save to produce plants like the mother plant, collect seeds only from nonhybrid varieties or cultivars. While you can save seeds from hybrids, the plants they produce won't look exactly like the mother plant

PROCEDURES

After the flowers from which you want to collect seeds finish blooming, don't deadhead them. Instead, leave them alone so that the seeds can mature. When the seed capsules or pods seem to be dry, break them off.

It's important to be certain that the seeds are dry before storing; moist seeds easily rot. Ensure this by picking the pods and placing them in paper bags (each kind in its own bag, labeled). Hang the bags in a warm, dry place to air-dry for two or three weeks. Shake the bags periodically. When the seeds are dry, separate them from their pods. Store them in small envelopes or paper bags that are labeled with the name of the plant, the flower color or other defining characteristic, and the harvest date.

Store the seeds in a cool, dry place. To be safe, place them in screw-top glass jars. Add a desiccant such as powdered milk or silica gel to the jar for a second layer of protection.

COLLECTING SEEDS

1 Cut or pick dried seedheads after the seeds have turned brown but before they drop to the ground.

2 After the seeds are completely dry, gently separate them from the seedhead with your fingers.

3 Pick out as many of the the seed coats and other large pieces of chaff as you can by hand.

4 Softly blow the remaining chaff away before storing the seeds in labeled bags or glass jars in a dry, cool area.

Gardens for dried arrangements

How are flowers dried?

Dried arrangements allow you to bring the glory of the blooming garden into the house for the winter. As you'll soon discover, a huge number of plants can be preserved by one method or another. Thin or stiff-petaled flowers and seedpods dry well almost on their own. All you have to do is pick them at the proper time and hang them upside down or stand them upright in a small amount of water to dry in the air. But there are several other ways to preserve flowers. The type of flower usually dictates which method works best. For example, the fleshy petals of a zinnia dry beautifully in silica gel, but if you want a softer look, preserve zinnias in glycerin. Even the microwave oven can be used to dry individual flowers.

Plan to grow some of the easily dried flowers and seedpods listed in the table on pages 50–51, but don't confine yourself to working with only those species. As you gain familiarity with preserving methods, you can experiment with other plants.

AIR-DRYING

Many of the plants we consider "everlasting" dry well in the air. Blooms such as perennial statice (Limonium species) and globe amaranth (Gomphrena globosa) are usually gathered just before the petals have fully opened, tied into small bunches, and hung upside down in a clean, dark spot with good ventilation. Depending on the species, the flowers will be dry in a few days to a week. There are only a few guidelines to follow with this method:

- The bunches should be small enough so that air can circulate around each bloom.

- The stems must be bunched so that the blooms are at different heights.

- The stems should be secured with a rubber band (which will automatically tighten as the stems lose water) or a twist tie that can be readjusted.

Some plants air-dry better in an upright position. Grasses, members of the onion family (Allium species), and annual statice all do well with this method. Use a tall container and stretch coarse netting or wire over the top. Place the stems through the netting so that the blooms are at different heights. Again, the best location to dry plants is a clean, dark place with good ventilation. (See the tips for drying plants upright.)

DRYING IN SILICA GEL

Silica gel is a desiccant that dries plants by gradually absorbing their moisture. It's used for such flowers as peonies, daffodils, and irises, which lose their petals, color, or shape when they are air-dried. It's always better to have too much rather than too little silica gel, so buy at least 5 pounds from a seed company or crafts supplier. Buy some duct tape, too; you'll need it to seal the lid.

Pick flowers for drying in silica gel when they first open fully and they are dry of rainwater or dew. Wire all flowers you plan to dry with silica gel because it makes the natural stems too brittle to work after they are dry. To save space in the drying container, attach a short wire to the flower, then extend the wire stem after the flowers are dried. Put an inch or so of silica gel in the bottom of the container with a tight-fitting lid, such as a cookie tin or plastic ice cream tub, and set the flowers on top of the material. Place daisy-shaped blooms face-down on the silica. Roses and trumpet-shaped blooms should be set face up. Leave an inch or so of space around each bloom. Gently sift more silica gel onto the flowers, shaking or pushing it down into creases as necessary, until the blooms are covered with about an inch of material. Now put the lid on, and tape it shut.

Air-dry flowers in a cool, dark location to retain the most vivid colors.

DRYING PLANTS UPRIGHT

If your plants wilt when you try to dry them in an upright position, you'll need to refine the technique. Stretch course netting or wire over the vase top to hold the stems in place, but add an inch of water to the bottom. Set the vase and plants in the drying area and let the water evaporate. The plants will dry more slowly than they would without water, but they will retain a fresher, fuller appearance.

Flossflower (*Ageratum* species), bells of Ireland (*Moluccella laevis*), baby's breath (*Gypsophila paniculata*), cockscomb (*Celosia cristata*) and yarrow (*Achillea filipendulina*) all dry well with this treatment.

REMOVING FLOWERS FROM SILCA GEL

Silica gel is heavy enough that it can damage your flowers if you yank them out of the containers. Instead, pour off the silica gel, a thin stream at a time, until most of your blooms are exposed. Use a soft brush to push the remaining silica gel away, and gently lift out the flowers.

DRYING IN THE MICROWAVE

Individual flowers can be dried in the microwave. It's best to do them one at a time, but if you become impatient with this, limit yourself to drying only two or three of the same kinds of flowers together. Prepare single flowers by inserting a wooden toothpick through the calyx. This will give you a hole to thread florists' wire through after the flower has dried.

Put an inch or so of silica gel in a microwave-safe bowl. Place the flowers or leaves on top of the silica gel, leaving about 1½ inches of space around each flower or leaf if working with more than one. Now sprinkle silica gel over the plant material, covering it to a depth of at least an inch.

Set the microwave at power level 4 if it goes from 1 to 10, or "defrost" if it doesn't. Timing varies with the plant, but if you are drying a single flower in approximately ½ pound of silica gel (the amount it takes to cover a bloom or two), begin with a setting of 2 ½ minutes. After the time is up, let the container stand for about 10 minutes for a single thin-petaled flower or leaf, and up to half an hour for a large flower such as a peony. (To prevent the dried material from reabsorbing moisture, put a lid on the container before you let it stand but leave it slightly cracked so that air can escape). After the standing time, gently pour off the silica gel and check to see that the material is dry. If not, recover it with silica gel and reheat it, always using cool silica gel.

As you gain experience with drying in the microwave, you'll learn how long each flower requires. Wait to wire them because if they reabsorb moisture while they are in storage, you may want to reheat them in the microwave.

HOW LONG DOES DRYING TAKE?

Drying time varies with species as well as the moisture content of the particular blooms you are drying. Three days in the silica gel should be adequate for quick-drying, thin-petaled flowers like cosmos, while fleshy blooms such as fuchsia and the like may take as long as two weeks. Check plants by tipping the container so that a few petals are exposed. Touch them. If they feel papery, they are probably dry enough. Even though you want the blooms to be completely dry, you do not want them to become brittle. As with so many other things in gardening, experience will be your best teacher. Once you have dried a few batches of flowers, you'll know how they should feel when they are completely dry.

Drying Wispy Stems with Multiple Florets. The directions above are best for large, single flowers. To dry flowering stems such as larkspur, wrap florists' wire

Drying flowers in silica

Place flowers at least an inch apart; this ensures the correct ratio between the material and the flowers. Almost any flower dries well in silica gel as long as you sift only an inch or so of the heavy material on top of the bloom. If it is piled too deeply, its weight will distort the shape of the flower.

DRY SILICA IN THE OVEN FOR REUSE

After you have removed your flowers, you will need to dry out your silica gel so that it can be reused. Some suppliers use a blue dye and some use a pink dye on some of the grains to indicate that the material is dry. You will notice these flecks when you open a new can of the material, but when you remove your blooms from it, the flecks will have disappeared. Dry the gel by putting it in a wide, shallow pan in a 250°F oven for about half an hour. Stir it occasionally to expose all of the material to the air. When it is dry, the blue or pink flecks will have returned. Store the material in an airtight container, taped shut, until the next time.

Position plants in a dried flower garden as you do those in a cutting garden. Plant in rows and arrange them by cultural requirements.

around the entire stem of the plant, and place it in a tall, narrow plastic container with a lid. Pour in the silica gel very slowly so the florets are not injured in the process. You can also dry these stems flat if you have a long, shallow container. Cover the container securely, and tape it closed for best results.

PRESERVING WITH GLYCERIN

Glycerin is used to preserve whole branches of fairly mature leaves, as well as individual leaves and a few selected flowers. It has the advantages of making preserved plants more pliable than they might otherwise be, giving foliage a waxy look, and maintaining or enhancing colors.

Buy glycerin from a pharmacy, or if you are using large quantities, from a chemical supply company. Mix one part glycerin to two parts of simmering water that is just off the boil, stirring to mix thoroughly. Cool the solution

to room temperature before using, or it will cook your plants.

Whole branches or stems will preserve best if they are harvested in late summer rather than autumn. Cut your material in late morning after a few sunny, dry days.

Dry Stems Upright. Most stems and branches should be preserved in an upright position. Fill a tall, narrow container with about two inches of glycerin solution. Then stand the freshly cut stems in it, and put the container and stems in a cool, dark place. Check the container every day to make certain that the stems still have a supply of glycerin to draw into themselves. Most plants take from two days to a month to fully absorb the glycerin, but once they have absorbed it, the leaves will feel waxy; their color may have changed or darkened; and their veins will have darkened. Remove them as soon as the appearance has changed.

Preserve baby's breath by standing the stems in glycerin for three or four days, then hanging them upside down for a few days. The flowers will turn a lovely creamy color, and the stems will be pliable to use in arrangements. Both Chinese lanterns and statice should stand in a glycerin solution for two days, then be hung upside down for another two days. Bells-of-Ireland should be completely immersed in a glycerin solution for two or three days, then hung upside down for a day or so to allow the extra solution to drip off.

ARRANGING DRIED MATERIALS

Making winter bouquets and arrangements can fill many a stormy day. You can not only decorate your own home but also make wreaths and bouquets as gifts.

Let your creativity take hold when you arrange your dried flowers. Using some florist wire, florist tape, and florist foam, you'll be able to arrange your materials in almost any shape you desire. However, if you are mixing glycerin-preserved branches with air- or silica-dried materials, make certain that the arrangement is loose enough to allow air to circulate through so the flowers don't pick up moisture from one another. You'll also want to check periodically to wipe off any excess moisture. But aside from this precaution, you can mix and match your dried materials to your heart's content. Enjoy them, and discard them when they fade.

STORING DRIED MATERIALS

If you don't plan to arrange your dried flowers right away, you can store them. They last a year or two depending on the material. Ideal storage containers and conditions vary, depending on how the material was dried.

For air-dried material, large, shallow boxes similar to those florists use for long-stemmed roses, are generally the best containers. Sprinkle silica gel in the bottom, and cover it with clean paper towels. Now make small bunches of your dried material, and wrap each bunch in tissue paper. Put a single layer in the box, with the bunch

Wiring stems

Stems of some flowers become so brittle when they are dry that they crack and fall off as soon as you try to arrange them. You can avoid this problem by wiring the flowers. Wiring methods depend on the weight of the flower. Strawflowers, for example, dry well with only one wire, while the roses demand two. For strawflowers, cut a 6-inch length of florist wire for each bloom. Stick one end through the calyx, and bend it around itself to form a new stem. Or pierce the bottom of the center of the flower with one end of the wire; bend it into a hook; and draw it back down into the center of the bloom. For heavy flowers, stick the two wires through the calyx and bend the wires around themselves to make the new stem.

Once the bloom has dried, the calyx will have dried around the wire. If you need a longer piece of wire, you can add more wire to the original piece. Use green florist tape to cover the wire.

Use florist wire to make a stem for heavy flowers.

Wire snips or needle-nosed pliers speed your work.

CREATING DRIED-FLOWER ARRANGEMENTS

1 Attach the first layer of material to a wreath form using florist wire.

2 Use florist wire to attach individual leaves and flowers to the frame. Work around the frame to keep the design well balanced.

3 If you can't attach a bloom with wire, use a drop of hot glue to secure it. Place the glue so that it is hidden.

4 Hang the wreath in a cool location that receives indirect light to keep it looking fresh for a long time. You may need to gently dust it from time to time to keep it looking its best.

tops and bottoms alternating (just the way you keep shoes in a box). Cover the box, and put it in a dark, dry spot. Check the material every month to deter-mine whether it's reabsorbing moisture. If it is, add more silica gel to the box.

Material that was dried in silica gel must be stored in airtight plastic or tin containers. Sprinkle some silica gel in the bottom of the container; then add your dried material. Seal the lid with duct tape, and place it in a cool, dark spot. Store microwave-dried flowers alone or with flowers that have been dried in silica gel.

Glycerin-preserved materials release moisture in storage. Wipe leaves and flowers with a dish towel; then set them upright in tall cans or jars in a well ventilated area.

EASY-DRY FLOWERS AND SEED PODS

This table lists many of the most commonly grown annuals and biennials for drying. The various methods for preserving are described in detail on pages 45–49.

Name	Common	Ht	Season	Color	Soil
Anethum graveolens	Dill	1'–3'	Mid-late summer	Brown	Versatile
Amaranthus caudatus	Love-lies-bleeding	3'–5'	Late summer	Brick red	Versatile
Ammobium alatum	Winged everlasting	2'	Mid-late summer	Silver-white	Light, rich, sandy
Artemisia annua	Sweet Annie	2'–5'	Summer	Green	Well-drained
Carthamus tinctorius	Safflower	3'	Mid-late summer	Orange, white, yellow	Versatile
Celosia cristata	Cockscomb	1'–2'	Summer	Range	Rich, deep,
Celosia plumosa	Plumed celosia	2'	Mid-late summer	Maroon & pink or yellow	Well-drained
Centaurea cyanus	Bachelors button	2'–3'	Summer	Blue, pink, purple	Well-drained
Centaurea moschata	Sweet sultan	2'–3'	Summer	Pink, white	Well-drained
Consolida regalis	Larkspur	2'–3'	Summer	Range, brown	Well-drained fertile
Gomphrena globosa	Globe thistle	1½'	Summer	Range	Moist
Helianthus annuus	Sunflower	3'–10'	Summer	Range	Well-drained fertile
Helichrysum bracteatum	Strawflower	2'–4'	Summer	Range	Versatile
Lepidium densiflorum	Peppergrass	2'	Late summer	Yellow	Versatile
Helipterum roseum	Acroclinium	1½'	Summer	Range	Well-drained fertile
Papaver rhoea	Shirley poppy	1'–1½'	Late summer	White, red, pink	Versatile
Salvia spp.	Ornamental sage	1'–3'	Summer	Range	Well-drained fertile
Scabiosa stellata	Ping-Pong scabiosa	1'–1½'	Late summer	Pale pink to tan	Well-drained
Tithonia rotundifolia	Mexican flower	2'–6'	Summer	Orange, yellow	Well-drained
Viola spp.	Viola, pansy	6"–9"	Spring	Range	Well-drained
Zinnia spp.	Zinnia	1'–3'	Summer	Range	Well-drained

Exposure	Comments	Preserve
Full sun	Harvest before seeds drop to avoid volunteers.	Hang-dry
Full sun	Harvest after first seeds form	Stand upright
Full sun	Cut before centers are visible but after buds begin to open. Cut buds will not open.	Wire stems; air-dry
Full sun	Harvest stems when flowers form; will become a weed if seeds dry and drop	Hang-dry
Full sun	Harvest open blossoms.	Hang-dry
Full sun	Harvest when almost open. Stand upright in water that you allow to evaporate until dry.	Hang-dry
Full sun	Harvest when just open.	Remove foliage and hang-dry
Full sun	Harvest when three-quarters of the blooms are open.	Hang-dry
Full sun	Harvest when three-quarters of the blooms are open.	Hang-dry
Full sun	Dry flowers when bottoms bloom open; use seedpods too.	Hang-dry
Full sun	Harvest when almost fully open.	Hang-dry
Full sun	Harvest when just open.	Silica gel
Full sun	Harvest before fully open.	Wire stems, dry upright
Full sun	Harvest when seedpods have formed but before they open	Hang-dry
Full sun	Harvest when just beginning to open.	Hang-dry, glycerine
Full sun to part shade	Harvest pods when fully formed and almost dry.	Hang-dry
Full sun	Harvest when just beginning to open.	Hang-dry, glycerine
Full sun	You can wait to harvest until blooms are almost dry.	Stand upright
Full sun	Harvest when just open.	Sllica gel
Full sun	Harvest when just open.	Silica gel
Full sun	Harvest when just open.	Silica gel

A-Z of favorite annuals

AGERATUM

Ageratum houstonianum
Flossflower

These mostly low-growing plants form compact mounds of dark green leaves nearly covered with clusters of small, fluffy purple-blue, pink, or white flowers. Although the short varieties are the most widely grown, there are some taller cultivars too.

Hardiness: Tender.

Blooming Time: Early summer until frost.

Height: 6 inches to 2½ feet.

Spacing: 6 to 10 inches.

Light: Full sun to light shade; afternoon shade in Zones 7 and warmer.

Soil: Average to fertile, well-drained soil.

Moisture: Even, abundant moisture; does not tolerate dryness.

Garden Uses: Dwarf cultivars are favorites for edging flower beds, using in designs where a low element is needed, and in containers and window boxes.

Grow the taller cultivars in the middle of beds and borders or grow them in a cutting garden. The taller cultivars, especially, make good cut flowers.

Cut flowers when about half the blossoms on the stem are open. The best times to cut are in the morning or early evening. Condition the flowers before you arrange them by standing the stems in warm water almost to the base of the flowers. Leave them in the water for several hours. Remove all leaves that would be below the water level in the vase.

In bouquets and arrangements, the puffy little clusters of flossflower blossoms make good fillers to place between larger, more dramatic flowers. They last about a week in the vase.

Comments: Sow seeds indoors about 10 weeks before the last expected frost. The plants can't tolerate frost, so do not

'Royal Hawaii'

plant them out until the weather has settled in spring.

Deadhead regularly to keep plants looking neat and to encourage continued heavy blooming throughout the season. If some plants exhaust themselves in midsummer, remove and replace them. A good layer of mulch will help the plants withstand hot, dry conditions.

Flossflowers are prone to fungus disease problems. To decrease the chance of infection, water plants at ground level rather than with overhead hoses or sprinklers. If you do use an overhead watering system, water in the morning or early enough in the evening so that plants have time to dry off before dark.

Recommended Cultivars:

Good cultivars for cutting:

- 'Blue Horizon', 2 to 2 ½ ft.; blue flowers; tolerates heat
- 'Red Top', 2 to 2 ½ ft.; purple-red flowers
- 'White Bouquet', 2 to 2 ½ ft.; white flowers

Smaller cultivars:

- 'Blue Mink', 10–18 in.; powder blue flowers
- 'Blue Lagoon', 8 in.; light blue flowers
- 'Bavaria', 1 ft.; blue-and-white bicolored flowers
- Hawaii hybrids, 8 in.; medium blue, rosy purple, and white flowers

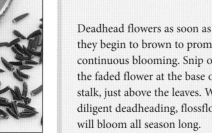
Flossflower seeds

DEADHEADING

Deadhead flowers as soon as they begin to brown to promote continuous blooming. Snip off the faded flower at the base of its stalk, just above the leaves. With diligent deadheading, flossflowers will bloom all season long.

AMARANTHUS

Amaranthus caudatus
Love-lies-bleeding
Amaranthus tricolor,
Joseph's-coat

Both of these amaranths have long, drooping, deep red flower spikes that look rather like chenille ropes. Joseph's-coat boasts colorful leaves of red, yellow, orange, bronze, and/or brown. All Amaranthus species are bushy and branched with oval leaves.

Hardiness: Tender.

Blooming Time: Summer.

Height: 1 to 4 feet.

Spacing: 1 ½ to 2 feet.

Light: Full sun.

Soil: Well-drained, average to poor fertility. Leaves of Joseph's-coat are less colorful in rich, fertile soils.

Moisture: Average; tolerates some dryness.

Garden Uses: These plants work best in the middle ground of a garden of large plants or in the back of a small garden of smaller plants. They also grow well in containers. The cultivars of A. caudatus and A. hypochondriacus are both good for cutting.

Comments: Amaranths are easy to grow but transplant best as young seedlings. Sow seeds indoors eight to ten weeks before the last expected frost, or direct-sow when frost danger is past. Both of these Amaranthus species grow best in warm weather.

Recommended Cultivars: A. tricolor:
- 'Illumination', 4 ft.; bright red leaves topped with yellow
- 'Summer Poinsettia Mix', 3 ft.; deep/bright red leaves
- 'Aurora', green leaves topped by chartreuse and yellow
- 'Joseph's Coat', 3 ft.; scarlet, cream, and green leaves
- A. caudatus: 'Green Thumb', 2 ft.; green leaves and vivid green flowers
- A. hypochondriacus, (or prince's feather, which has flower spikes that stand upright rather than drooping) 'Pygmy Torch', 1 to 2 ft.; upright wine red flower spikes

'Illumination'

SUPPORTING AMARANTHUS

Tomato cages make excellent supports for bushy, many-stalked species such as these love-lies-bleeding plants. Set cages in place before the plants begin to lean.

Joseph's-coat

ANTIRRHINUM

Antirrhinum majus
Snapdragon

The colorful spikes of snapdragons are a fine addition to any garden. They add a colorful vertical accent, are wonderful for cutting, and have been favorites of generations of children. The plants may be either annual or perennial, but they are usually grown as annuals.

Hardiness: Half-hardy.

Blooming Time: Early summer; in warm climates, winter or early spring.

Height: 9 inches to 3 feet, depending on cultivar.

Spacing: 6 inches to 1 foot, depending on cultivar.

Light: Full sun to partial shade; prefers some afternoon shade in warm climates.

Soil: Well-drained, moderately rich.

A group of snapdragons in pastel hues softens the appearance of these steps and stone wall.

Moisture: Evenly moist.

Garden Uses: Grow snapdragons in beds, borders, or cutting gardens.

Seed leaves

Comments: Snapdragons grow best in cool weather. In Zones 3 to 6, start seeds indoors 8 to 12 weeks before the last expected spring frost and set out seedlings as soon as the soil can be worked. In Zones 9 and warmer, sow in fall. Seeds need light to germinate; do not cover them. To extend the blooming period, sow seeds in batches several weeks apart. Deadheading faded flower spikes helps prolong bloom. If you cut off entire spikes when the flowers fade, plants may rebloom in fall.

Recommended Cultivars:

• 'Bright Butterflies', 2 ½ ft.; red, pink, bronze, yellow, white flowers

• 'Sonnet Mix', 1 ½ ft.; shades of red/pink, yellow/bronze, white flowers

• 'Floral Showers Mix', 6–8 in.; red, pink, purple, orange, yellow, white, lavender-and-white bicolored flowers; blooms early in season

• 'Floral Carpet Mixed', 8 in.; red, pink, yellow, white

• Rocket hybrids, 2 ½–3 ft.; various shades of red, pink, bronze, yellow, and white flowers

Rocket hybrids

Snapdragons make excellent garden companions for pansies.

ARGYRANTHEMUM

Argyranthemum frutescens (Chrysanthemum frutescens)
Marguerite

Marguerites have dainty, daisylike flowers a couple of inches across. The centers are golden, but the petals may be white, yellow, or pink. Some cultivars have densely packed, small upright petals around the center that can completely obscure the true disk flowers. The plants are branched and bushy, with finely divided, rather lacy-looking leaves.

Hardiness: Tender.

Blooming Time: All summer if deadheaded regularly.

Height: 1 to 3 feet.

Spacing: 1 to 1 ½ feet.

Light: Full sun.

Soil: Well-drained, average fertility.

Moisture: Average; water when soil is dry.

Garden Uses: Marguerites are durable plants for container gardens and window boxes as well as garden beds and borders. They perform beautifully as long as they receive regular deadheading throughout the season.

Comments: Marguerites were formerly grouped under Chrysanthemum but have been reclassified by botanists as *Argyranthemum frutescens*. But because some suppliers still list them as Chrysanthemum, shop for them under that name too if you can't find them as Argyranthemum.

'Pink Lady'

Recommended Cultivars:

- 'Butterfly', 1 ½ ft.; yellow flowers
- 'Vancouver', 1 ½–2 ft.; double pink flowers with dense "anemone" centers surrounded by narrow, widely spaced rays

'Silver Lady'

Single marguerites

DEADHEADING MARGUERITE

Deadhead flowers as soon as they begin to fade. With regular deadheading, most marguerites will continue to bloom all summer.

BEGONIA

Begonia Semperflorens-Cultorum hybrids
Wax begonia

Wax begonias have glossy, rounded leaves 2 to 4 inches long in varying shades of green and bronze. As a rule, green-leaved cultivars can tolerate more shade than bronze-leaved types. The inch-wide flowers can be either single or double (depending on the cultivar) and can come in shades of pink and red as well as white.

Hardiness: Tender.

Blooming Time: All summer into fall.

Height: 6 inches to 1 foot.

Spacing: 6 inches to 1 foot.

Light: Best in light shade; tolerates full sun in cooler climates. Plants will grow in medium to full shade but will produce fewer flowers.

Soil: Well-drained, fertile, rich in organic matter.

Moisture: Evenly moist.

Garden Uses: Wax begonias are excellent bedding plants and work beautifully in window boxes and containers. They make good houseplants, too. In autumn, before the first frost, you can dig up plants or take cuttings to root and pot up for winter bloom indoors.

Comments: To start wax begonias from seed, sow seeds indoors in January or February. Seeds are very fine; scatter them as evenly as you can over the surface of a fine-textured potting medium and press them in gently. Keep the soil moist, with lots of light and temperatures between 65° and 80°F. Transplant to the garden after the frost-free date.

Because wax begonia plants are so slow to reach blooming size from seed, many gardeners find it easier to purchase plants at local garden centers.

Bronze-leaved cultivars tolerate more sun than green-leaved, and variegated ones and are better choices for sunny locations and gardens in Zones 7 and warmer.

Recommended Cultivars:
- Ambassador hybrids, 8 in.; green leaves; red, pink, white, red-and-white bicolored flowers; early blooming
- Cocktail hybrids, 6 in.; bronze leaves, red, pink, white flowers
- Lotto hybrids, 8 in.; green leaves; red and pink flowers
- Senator series, 8 in.; early blooming; bronze leaves; flowers in two shades of rose, pink, white, and scarlet

ROOTING CUTTINGS

Take cuttings from established plants in late summer to root for winter houseplants. You can also take cuttings in late winter, root them, and set them out once the spring weather has settled.

- Super Olympia series replaces the older Olympia hybrids; early blooming; green leaves; flowers in red, coral, pink, white, and a rose-and-white bicolor
- Varsity series, to 9 in.; early blooming; good in the Northeast; green leaves; flowers in shades of scarlet, rose, pink, and white, as well as rose-and-white bicolor

Wax begonias in mixed colors

BROWALLIA

Browallia speciosa
Sapphire flower

Sapphire flower plants bear star-shaped, violet-blue blooms about 2 inches across on branching stems with small, bright green, lance-shaped leaves. The compact plants have a bushy form.

Hardiness: Tender.

Blooming Time: Summer.

Height: 8 inches to 1 foot.

Spacing: 10 inches to 1 foot.

Light: Partial to light shade; full sun in cool climates.

Soil: Well-drained; average fertility, but not too rich.

Moisture: Needs abundant moisture.

Garden Uses: An underused plant in most gardens, sapphire flower is delightful for edging beds and borders or for growing in containers, window boxes, and hanging baskets.

Comments: Grows best in fairly warm weather. Sow seeds indoors six to eight weeks before the last expected frost. Do not cover seeds. Overfertilization results in fewer blooms.

Browallia

Recommended Cultivars:
- 'Blue Bells', 8–12 in.; blue flowers
- 'Jingle Bells', to 1 ft.; flowers in mixed colors
- 'Silver Bells', 8–12 in.; white flowers

Propagating

Browallia cuttings root faster when the end of the cutting is dipped in rooting hormone powder before planting. To avoid contaminating the hormone with a disease organism, shake some powder into another container and discard the excess after you use it.

WINTER FLOWERS

Sapphire flowers make excellent winter houseplants. Take cuttings from established plants in late summer, and root for winter houseplants.

CALENDULA

Calendula officinalis
Pot marigold

Calendulas produce golden yellow, orange, or cream-colored daisylike flowers on bushy, branching plants with narrow, oblong, somewhat coarse-textured green leaves. Some cultivars have full, double-petaled flowers.

Hardiness: Hardy.

Blooming Time: Early summer to fall, winter in warm climates.

Height: 1 to 2 feet.

Spacing: 10 inches to 1 foot.

Light: Full sun.

Soil: Well-drained, average fertility.

Moisture: Average; water during dry spells.

Garden Uses: Plant these sunny flowers near the front or middle of a bed or in containers. They also make good cut flowers.

Comments: Calendulas grow best in cool weather and can tolerate some frost; plant in early spring as soon as they become available from garden centers. Start seeds indoors eight weeks before the last expected frost and transplant a week or two before the frost-free date. Or sow seeds outdoors as soon as you can work the soil. In warm climates, plant seeds in fall for winter flowers.

Calendulas are easy to grow and have herbal as well as decorative uses. The edible flower petals can be used fresh as a garnish or salad ingredient, or they can be dried and used as a substitute for saffron, to add color to rice dishes, or as a skin-soothing addition to homemade soaps or salves.

Recommended Cultivars:
- 'Bon Bon', 1 ft.; orange and yellow flowers
- 'Fiesta', 1 ft.; yellow, orange, bicolored flowers
- 'Pacific Beauty', 1 ½ ft.; shades of yellow to red-orange

Calendulas

CUTTING BACK FOR REGROWTH

1 When spring-planted calendulas begin to fatigue in midsummer, it's time for a rejuvenation treatment.

2 Cut back the plants to leave at least one set of leaves and stems a few inches high. Use pruning clippers or flower shears.

3 The cut-back plants will send out new growth and a fresh crop of flowers in late summer and fall.

CALLISTEPHUS

Callistephus chinensis
China aster

These popular cutting flowers are native to China and Japan. Many cultivars of China asters are available, giving a choice of heights and bloom times. Flowers can be white, purple, blue-violet, and various shades of pink and rosy red.

Hardiness: Tender.

Blooming Time: Summer into fall.

Height: 9 inches to 2 feet.

Spacing: 1 to 1 ½ feet.

Light: Full sun.

Soil: Average to rich, well-drained.

Moisture: Average; water during dry spells.

Garden Uses: Grow in the front to middle of beds and borders, cutting gardens, or in containers.

Comments: To avoid building up populations of the diseases that strike asters, do not grow them in the same area of the garden where they grew during the previous two or three years. For an instant bouquet, cut the whole plant; though the color will be uniform, the branch arrangement will be graceful.

Where the growing season is short, start seeds indoors about six weeks before the last expected spring frost. Elsewhere, sow outdoors after all danger of frost has passed.

Recommended Cultivars:

- 'Dwarf Queen', 8 in.; double flowers of red, scarlet, rose pink, blue, white
- 'Mini Lady', 10 in.; large double flowers of scarlet, rose, blue, white; early blooming
- 'Milady Mixed', 10–12 in.; scarlet, rose, pink, blue, and white flowers
- 'Massagno Mixed', 1 ½ ft.; spider-type blossoms with long, thin petals in shades of red, pink, purple, white
- 'Galaxy Mix', 2 ft.; yellow centers with pink, purple, and white spoon-shaped petals
- 'Mixed Powder-puffs', many colors

Mixed China asters

'Milady Blue'

RECUTTING STEMS

When using China asters as cut flowers, recut their stems underwater before arranging them in a vase. Recut every two days to keep them fresh.

'Ostrich Plume'

CATHARANTHUS

Catharanthus roseus
Madagascar periwinkle, Vinca

Parasol

Madagascar periwinkle in mixed colors

Madagascar periwinkles are known for their white or rosy pink five-petaled flowers, some with a deep pink eye. The flowers are set off by glossy, dark green leaves.

Hardiness: Hardy.

Blooming Time: All summer into fall.

Height: 6 inches to 2 feet.

Spacing: 8 inches to 1 foot.

Light: Full sun.

Soil: Well-drained, average fertility.

Moisture: Evenly moist.

Garden Uses: A good plant for containers or the front to middle of beds and borders.

Comments: Purchase Madagascar periwinkle plants from garden centers because they are difficult to grow from seed. If you do try to start them, keep the medium at 80° to 85°F and cover the flat; the seeds need darkness to germinate. These plants love heat and humidity. Do not transplant until the soil has warmed in spring. They cannot tolerate cool temperatures. Vinca doesn't perform well where summers are cool; the leaves can turn yellow if the plant is exposed to cold temperatures. Cultivars in the Cooler series perform better in cooler conditions than other types do. Newer cultivars are tolerant of high winds and heavy rain. They are also self-cleaning, meaning that old blossoms drop off by themselves; you do not need to deadhead these plants. Madagascar periwinkle is perennial in Zones 9 and warmer.

Recommended Cultivars:
- Cooler series, slightly over 1 ft.; white, pink, orchid, rose flowers; some with a contrasting eye
- Pacifica series, 1 ft.; large flowers of white, pink, apricot-pink, lilac, red, most with a contrasting eye
- 'Parasol', 15 in.; largest flowers; white with a red eye
- Tropicana series, rose, pink, white; contrasting eye

Taking cuttings
After taking cuttings from established plants, remove the flowers and strip the bottom leaves so that you can bury at least two nodes in the soil mix.

CELOSIA

Celosia argentea
Woolflower, Cockscomb

'Flamingo Feather'

A varied species, Celosia offers flowerheads in feathery plumes, loose spires, or a variety of bizarre curled, crested, and fan shapes, some resembling twisted corals, brains, or deformed rooster's combs. Traditionally, the flowers have bloomed in bright, hot colors—red, magenta, scarlet, rose, pink, orange, and yellow—but now there are cultivars in softer shades of gold, yellow, apricot, and cream, particularly among the plume group (often sold as Celosia plumosa). All species are upright with a branching to bushy form and oval leaves.

Hardiness: Tender.

Blooming Time: All summer.

Height: 6 inches to 3 feet.

Spacing: 1 to 2 feet, depending on type. Smaller-growing cultivars can be planted at the closer spacing; larger ones farther apart.

Light: Full sun; afternoon shade in warm climates.

Soil: Any good garden soil.

Moisture: Average to damp.

Garden Uses: The traditional brilliant colors of cockscombs are difficult to mix with other flowers and are best surrounded with white flowers, silver-gray foliage (like that of artemisias or dusty millers) or lots of green leaves. The newer cultivars with softer colors are easier to work with and can be quite pretty with other warm-toned blooms. Use smaller cultivars in the front of the garden, taller types in the middle ground, or grow in containers. The flowers are good for cutting and drying.

Comments: The plants can't tolerate cold, so don't plant them out in the garden until the soil has warmed in spring. Sow indoors a month before the last expected frost.

Recommended Cultivars:

Plume group:

- 'Apricot Brandy', 1 to 1 ½ ft.; apricot-orange flowers
- Castle series, 1 ft.; rosy pink, scarlet, yellow flowers
- Century series, 2 ft.; red, rose, yellow, cream flowers

Plume type

Cockscomb group:

- 'Big Chief Mixed', slightly over 3 ft.; red, scarlet, yellow flowers
- 'Jewel Box Improved', 6 in.; red, pink, orange, salmon, white flowers, plus bicolored
- 'Prestige Scarlet', 1 to 1 ½ ft.; scarlet flowers
- C. spicata (known as wheat celosia) 'Flamingo Feather', 2 to 2 ½ ft.; feathery pink flower spikes that show white as they open

Staking

Heavy flowerheads of cockscomb celosia show to their best advantage when the plants are staked. Staking also keeps stems straight, an advantage if you cut them.

CENTAUREA

Centaurea cyanus
Bachelor's button, Cornflower

Bachelor's buttons are tall, slender plants with charming, old-fashioned-looking flowers. The sparse leaves and open habit can make the plants look weedy late in the season. Spiky, pointed petals are various shades of deep sky blue, light blue, pink, purple, red, deep maroon, and white.

Hardiness: Hardy.

Blooming Time: Summer.

Height: 1 to 3 feet.

Spacing: 6 inches to 1 foot.

Light: Full sun.

Soil: Well-drained.

Moisture: Average.

Garden Uses: Bachelor's buttons make delightful additions to cottage gardens, meadow gardens, and the middle of informal beds and borders. Cut blooms when they are almost fully open. If you recut stems every second day, they hold well for up to a week.

Comments: Deadhead regularly to prolong blooming. Plants often rebloom if cut back severely after the first bloom. To guarantee flowers all season, plant several successive sowings two to three weeks apart. Direct-seed in spring as soon as soil can be worked in cool climates, but in the fall in mild ones; grows best in cooler weather.

'Frosted Mix'

Deadhead flowers as soon as they begin to brown to promote continuous blooming.

Recommended Cultivars:

- 'Dwarf Midget Mix', 1 ft.; blue, pink, mauve, red, white
- 'Garnet', 2 ft.; burgundy flowers
- 'Polka Dot Mixed', 1 ½ ft.; blue, red, maroon, rosy pink, lavender, and white flowers

SAVING BACHELOR'S BUTTON SEED

1 Crush the seedheads with a heavy mallet to release the seeds.

2 Rub the seeds and chaff between your hands to further loosen the seeds.

3 Use a colander to separate the seeds from the large pieces of chaff.

CLEOME

Cleome hassleriana
Spider flower

This amazing-looking plant is among the tallest of annuals, growing up to 6 feet high in a single summer. Its distinctive flowers, with their long, waving stamens (which resemble the legs of the spiders children call "daddy longlegs") are gathered into loose, round clusters at the tops of the tall, upright stems.

Spider flower

Flowers come in shades of rose, pink, and purple, as well as white. The medium green leaves are deeply lobed and palm-shaped.

Hardiness: Half-hardy.

Blooming Time: All summer.

Height: 3 to 6 feet; not as tall when grown in containers or in less-than-optimum conditions.

Spacing: 1 to 2 feet.

Light: Full sun to partial shade.

Soil: Average, well-drained.

Moisture: Average; tolerates dry soil, but not prolonged drought.

Garden Uses: These tall plants are striking massed in the back of the garden, where they provide a strong vertical line. Or try spider flowers in the center or back of a tub garden of mixed flowers. The flowers are good for cutting.

Comments: Transplant spider flowers with care; they don't transplant very well. Or direct seed outdoors in spring, after the weather begins to warm but before all danger of frost is past.

The plants may self-sow, but self-sown plants will not grow as large as their parents. In warm climates, they can become invasive if left to go to seed. The tall stems may need staking in a windy garden.

Volunteer plants

Recommended Cultivars:

- 'Helen Campbell', 3 ft.; white flowers
- Queen series, 3 ft;, pink, rosy pink, lilac-purple flowers
- 'Color Fountain Mixed', 3–3 ½ ft.; pink, rose, purple, lilac, white flowers

STARTING SEEDS INDOORS

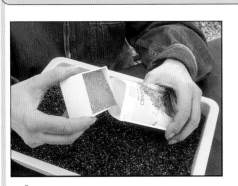

1 Add sand to the seed packet to make seeds easier to plant.

2 Tap out the seeds and sand mixture into furrows in the medium.

3 Use a mister to moisten the flat without disturbing seed placement.

COLEUS

Solenostemon scutellarioides
Coleus hybrids

Coleus

These branched, bushy plants are grown for their oval to lance-shaped leaves that come in various combinations of colors: green, chartreuse, red, maroon, white, pink, apricot, brown, and yellow. The leaves have toothed, scalloped, or frilled edges and a somewhat quilted texture. In summer the plants send up small spikes of little white or purple flowers; these detract from the plants' appearance and are best removed.

Hardiness: Tender.

Blooming Time: Mid- to late summer.

Height: 8 inches to 2 feet.

Spacing: 8 inches to 1 foot, depending on cultivar; set smaller-growing plants at the closer spacing.

Light: Partial to light shade; tolerates full sun. In full shade, plants will be smaller and less full; in full sun, the colors won't be as rich.

Soil: Average to fertile, rich in organic matter; tolerates a range of soil conditions.

Moisture: Needs even moisture, especially in dry weather.

Garden Uses: Coleus is a good source of color and mass in the front of a shady garden or in the middle ground of a bed of small plants. It also grows well in pots.

Comments: The plants are tender, so don't plant them in the garden until all danger of frost is past. Pinch back the tips of young stems to encourage bushier plants. Pinch off flowers when they begin to form to keep plants growing vigorously.

You can take stem cuttings at the end of summer and root them in water, then pot them up to grow as houseplants in winter. Coleus plants are perennial in Zones 10 and 11.

Recommended Cultivars:

- 'Wizard Mixed', 10 in.; large assortment of colors and combinations
- 'Rainbow Blend', 1 ½ ft., vigorous plants in a variety of colors and combinations
- Fiji series, serrated or deeply cut leaves in 11 different colors/combinations
- Old Lace series, 1 ½ ft.; ruffled, serrated, or deeply cut leaves in a range of colors and combinations
- Poncho series, cascading, for hanging baskets

Removing Flower Stalks

Flower stalks on coleus plants are often considered unattractive. Remove them to keep the plants looking neat and tidy.

ROOTING STEM CUTTINGS

1 Clip off healthy, 4 to 6-inch long stem tips for your cuttings.

2 Remove the lower leaves from each stem before inserting it into the water.

3 Plant the rooted cuttings in 4 to 6-inch pots in moist potting soil.

CONSOLIDA

C. ambigua (Consolida ajacis)
Rocket larkspur

Tall spikes of single or double flowers in violet, purple, blue, pink, and white grace these hardy plants. The flowering stems may be up to 4 feet tall.

Hardiness: Hardy.

Blooming Time: Late spring to early summer.

Height: 1 ½ to 4 feet.

Spacing: 10 inches to 1 foot.

Light: Full sun to partial shade.

Soil: Rich, fertile, well-drained.

Moisture: Evenly moist.

Garden Uses: These tall, graceful plants mix beautifully with peren-nials. Plant them in the middle or back of a bed or border, in a cottage garden, or wherever you need a strong vertical line. They make lovely cut flowers and also dry well.

Comments: Larkspur grows best in cool weather. Plant seeds directly in the garden. Plant in the fall in warm climates; where the ground freezes in winter, plant as soon as the soil can be worked in spring. You can also sow seeds indoors in individual peat pots (seeds need darkness to

Collecting seedpods

Wait to collect the seedpods until they have turned brown and have begun to dry. If you are concerned that the seeds will drop before you get them, twist-tie a paper bag around them before they are completely dry.

germinate). Transplant outdoors, with care, when the soil is workable. Larkspur does not transplant well, so move them before they become rootbound. Plants often self-sow if not deadheaded. Tall cultivars may need staking.

Recommended Cultivars:

- 'Earlibird Mixed', 1 ½–2 ft.; early blooming; double rose, lilac, blue, white flowers
- 'Kaleidoscope Mix', 1 ½–2 ft.; single to double vio-let-blue, lavender, rose, pink, white flowers
- 'King Size Mix', 1 ½–2 ft.; double rose, pink, salmon, carmine, lilac, blue, white flowers

Larkspur

Larkspurs give an excellent vertical accent at the back of a border.

CONVOLVULUS

Convolvulus tricolor
Dwarf morning-glory

Dwarf morning-glories are bushy and sprawl instead of climbing. The flowers look like smaller, fancier versions of the familiar vining morning-glories. The center of each blossom is yellow, a white zone surrounds it, and the remaining half of each petal is blue, purple, red, or pink.

Hardiness: Half-hardy.

Blooming Time: Late spring to late summer.

Height: to 2 feet and spreading.

Spacing: 10 inches to 1 foot.

Light: Full sun.

Soil: Average, well-drained.

Moisture: Evenly moist.

Garden Uses: Plant dwarf morning-glory in a hanging basket, let it ramble about the front of a bed or border, or plant it where it will tumble over the edge of a raised bed or retaining wall.

Comments: Abrade the hard seed coat with sandpaper, or soak the seeds overnight before planting. After danger of frost has passed, direct-seed outside. Or sow seeds early indoors in peat pots, and carefully transplant outdoors when the danger of frost is past.

Recommended Cultivars:

- Ensign series, 1–2-ft. spread; red, blue, rose, white flowers with a yellow eye and white throat
- 'Dwarf Picotee Mixed', 1 ft.; variegated leaves; red, pink, salmon, blue flowers edged in white

Dwarf morning-glory

PLANTING

Peat pots allow you to transplant morning-glory seedlings without disturbing their delicate roots.

Seed leaves

COSMOS

Cosmos species

Gold-centered daisylike flowers of crimson, rose, pink, and white (Cosmos bipinnatus) or scarlet, orange, gold, and yellow (C. sulphureus) are extraordinarily appealing in summer beds and borders. Cosmos foliage is finely divided and has a feathery appearance. The branching plants have a light, open texture. They sometimes look a bit weedy late in the season.

Hardiness: Tender.

Blooming Time: Midsummer until frost.

Height: 2 to 5 feet, depending on variety and growing conditions.

Spacing: 1 foot.

Light: Full sun is best; also grows reasonably well in partial shade.

Soil: Average fertility, tolerates poor soil; good drainage is essential.

Moisture: Tolerates some drought.

Garden Uses: Cosmos are wonderful, exuberant plants for the middle to the back of the garden, depending on the mature height of the cultivar. The flower colors combine beautifully with many other flowers. Cosmos hold up well in hot weather. The flowers are excellent for cutting.

Comments: In most climates, it's best to direct-seed. Where the frost-free season is short, start seeds early indoors in peat pots. Transplant to the garden after all danger of frost is past in spring, taking care not to disturb the roots.

Cultivars of C. bipinnatus bloom in groups of three flowers. When deadheading the first blooms, cut them off immediately below the flowerhead; two new buds will then form below the cut. After these flowers fade, deadhead by clipping off the stems at the next pair of leaves. Flowers of the yellow and orange species appear singly on long stems; cut back to the next pair of leaves when deadheading.

DEADHEADING COSMOS

Deadhead flowers as soon as the petals fade or begin to dry to encourage plants to bloom all summer. If you want the plants to self-seed, leave only a few faded flowers on the plant late in the summer.

Recommended Cultivars: C. bipinnatus:

- 'Gazebo', 4 ft.; crimson, lavender-pink, white flowers
- 'Early Wonder', 4 ½ ft.; crimson, rose, pink, white flowers
- 'Sonata', 1 ½–2 ft.; red, rose, pink, white flowers
- 'Versailles', 1 ½ to 2 ft.; red, white, shades of pink flowers
- 'Seashells', 3–3 ½ ft.; tubular petals of red, pink, cream
- 'Bright Lights', 3 ft.; early; semidouble scarlet, orange, gold, yellow flowers.
- C. sulphureus:
- 'Lady-bird' series, 1 ft.; red, yellow, and orange flowers
- 'Polidor Mix', 3 ft.; semidouble red, gold, orange flowers

'Seashells'

Bright lights mix

DIANTHUS

Dianthus chinensis
China pinks

China pinks are biennials or short-lived perennials that are usually grown as annuals. The clove-scented flowers come in shades of red, pink, white, and many bicolors, generally with a central, darker eye. The petals are fringed. The upright mounded plants have narrow bluish green leaves.

Hardiness: Hardy.

Blooming Time: Late spring to midsummer.

Height: 1 to 1 ½ feet.

Spacing: 6 inches to 1 foot.

Light: Full sun; some afternoon shade is helpful where summers are hot.

Soil: Average fertility; light, well-drained, sandy soil with a neutral to slightly alkaline pH.

SITING

Place China pinks where they will get some afternoon shade if you live in an area with hot summers. This is particularly important for plants growing in containers because they are so exposed when growing alone.

Cutting back

To get more blooms from the plants, perform this simple but important maintenance chore: cut back the stems after plants have finished their first bloom. The stems will regrow and reward you with a second bloom later in the season.

China pinks

'Raspberry Parfait'

Moisture: Average.

Garden Uses: Position China pinks in the front of the garden, or grow them in containers. They're charming in a cottage garden or rock garden as well.

Comments: Sow directly outdoors when frost danger is past, or start them indoors about 10 weeks before the last frost. Set plants with the crowns right at the soil surface; don't plant too deep.

Recommended Cultivars:

- Parfait series, 6 in.; flowers are small and weather-resistant and single or bicolored in shades of pink or light red
- Carpet series, 6 in.; red, white, bicolored single flowers
- Magic Charms series, 6 in.; red, coral, white, bicolored
- Princess series, 6 in.; red, salmon, pink, purple, white
- 'Black & White Minstrels', 6–10 in.; a deep purplish black-and-white bicolored bloom
- 'Color Magician', to 10 in.; small, single flowers that change from white to pink to rose-pink as they age

GOMPHRENA

Gomphrena globosa
Globe amaranth

Rounded flowerheads resembling clover blossoms grace globe amaranth plants. The oval leaves grow on stiff, branching stems. Flower colors include red-violet, red, pink purple, lavender, and white. The related G. haageana expands the color range to orange shades.

Hardiness: Tender.

Blooming Time: Summer into fall.

Height: 8 inches to 2 feet.

Spacing: 10 inches to 1 ½ feet.

Light: Full sun; tolerates partial shade.

Soil: Well-drained, average to poor fertility.

Moisture: Average, tolerates drought.

Garden Uses: Grow globe amaranth in containers or in the front of beds and borders. The flowers dry beautifully; cut them while the flower heads are still round, before they open fully.

Globe amaranth

Hang the flowers upside down in bunches in a dry, airy location to air-dry. The stems become rather brittle when dried and will hold up better in arrangements if you first wrap them with green florist wire to brace them. You can hide the wire with green florist tape if necessary.

To use globe amaranth as a fresh-cut flower, remove the lower leaves and place the stems in a container of water almost up to the base of the flowers for several hours before arranging them.

Comments: Direct-seed in the garden when frost danger is past, or start seeds indoors about six weeks before the last frost. Soak seeds overnight or for a day or two before you sow them. Globe amaranth holds up well in hot, dry summer weather.

Recommended Cultivars:

- 'Bicolor Rose', 2 ft.; lilac flowers with white centers
- 'Dwarf Buddy', 6 in.; purple flowers
- 'Lavender Lady', 2 ft.; lavender flowers

Globe amaranth seeds

- 'Woodcreek Mixed', 1 ½ ft.; red, rose, pink, orange, lilac, purple, white flowers
- 'Strawberry Fields', 2 ½ ft.; red flowers to 2 in. long
- 'Dwarf White', 6 in.; long-lasting white flowers

CUTTING GOMPHRENA

Cut globe amaranth flowers for drying while the petals are still tight. Hang upside down in bunches to air-dry in an airy, sheltered location.

HELIANTHUS

Helianthus annuus
Sunflower

These tall golden flowers are easy to grow and long-blooming. The most common sunflowers are golden yellow, but lately the palette has expanded. Particular cultivars may also bloom in shades of orange, mahogany, maroon, and cream. Some have large brown centers. This species includes the giant sunflower that provides seeds for birds and human snackers; its flowers can easily grow to 1 foot across. Most cultivars are tall, upright, branched plants with large, coarse leaves.

Hardiness: Hardy.

Blooming Time: Mid- to late summer.

Height: 2½ to 7 feet (10 or even 12 feet is common for the giant sunflower).

Spacing: 1 to 2 feet.

Light: Full sun to partial shade.

Soil: Well-drained, average fertility.

Moisture: Evenly moist; tolerates some dryness.

Garden Uses: Sunflowers are cheerful, lively plants that are most at home in informal gardens; most are too coarse for formal beds and borders. Dwarf cultivars are the most versatile; all but the smallest sunflowers belong in the back of the garden. Giant sunflowers can be planted in a row; their tall, straight stems will form a border or light screen.

Comments: Sunflowers grow best in warm weather, but they are reasonably hardy when established. Direct-seed when all danger of frost is past in the spring.

'Music Box'

Recommended Cultivars:

- 'Mammoth Russian', 12 ft.; golden flower, yellow center
- 'Valentine', 5 ft.; pale lemon yellow flowers with dark centers
- 'Sonja', 3 ½ ft.; deep orange flowers
- 'Italian White', 5–7 ft; cream flowers with dark centers
- 'Music Box', 2 ½–3 ft.; mixed flower colors—yellow shades to red

SAVING SUNFLOWER SEEDS

1 Sunflower pollen is large and quite visible when it is ready to fertilize the seeds. Both wind and insects pollinate sunflowers.

2 After the pollen has dropped and the seeds have been fertilized, the seeds begin to develop. They become larger as the days go by.

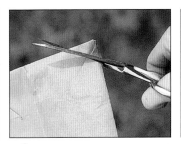

3 Prepare a paper bag for covering the seedhead by cutting off one corner so that any rainwater that gets into it can also drip out.

4 The bag prevents birds from eating the seeds. Staple it around the stem with the cut corner positioned at the lowest point.

HELICHRYSUM

Helichrysum bracteatum
Strawflower
Helichrysum petiolare
Licorice plant

Strawflowers (H. bracteatum) produce papery-petaled blossoms in warm shades of red, orange, yellow, pink, and creamy white. The branching plants have narrow, oblong leaves. Some references now list these plants as Bracteantha bracteatum.

Licorice plant (H. petiolare) is a low sprawling plant with small, rounded, fuzzy, silvery gray-green leaves with a mild licorice scent. These plants are perennial in Zones 10 and 11.

Hardiness: Half-hardy.

Blooming Time: Summer into autumn.

Height: Strawflower, 1 ½ to 3 feet; licorice plant, 1 ½ feet.

Spacing: 8 to 14 inches.

Light: Full sun.

Soil: Well-drained, average.

Moisture: Average, let soil dry between waterings; tolerates dry conditions.

Garden Uses: Strawflowers are excellent for drying and can be used in fresh arrangements, too. Plant them in the cutting garden or in the middle to the back of beds and borders.

Licorice plant blends with most flower colors. It is delightful cascading over the edge of a mixed container or hanging basket and works well in the front of a bed or mixed border.

Comments: Direct-seed when all danger of frost is past in spring and the soil is warm. Or start indoors about six weeks before the last expected frost. Seeds need light to germinate; press into the soil surface.

Cut strawflowers for drying before they are fully open. Strawflower stems are brittle and break easily; avoid problems by replacing them with florist wire. Right after you cut the flowers, poke a length of florist wire through the center of each; make a small hook in the end of the wire that you pushed through the flower; and then draw it back down into the center of the blossom so that it's invisible. Dry the flowers by sticking the wires into Styrofoam in a dark place with good

Licorice plant

air circulation. The wire allows you to arrange the flowers once they're dry.

Recommended Cultivars:

H. bracteatum:

- 'Bright Bikini Mix', 1 ft.; red, pink, yellow, white flowers
- 'Fiery Mix', red, orange, yellow, white flowers
- 'Victorian Pastels', to 4 ft.; pink, salmon, white flower
- 'Monstrosum', 21/2 ft.; red, rose, orange, purple, white flowers

H. petiolare:

- 'Limelight', chartreuse leaves
- 'Variegatum', variegated with creamy white markings

CUTTING STRAWFLOWERS FOR DRYING

Cut flowers for drying right below the calyx because the stems are too brittle to retain.

Strawflowers

HELIOTROPIUM

Heliotropium arborescens
Heliotrope

These shrubby plants are loved for their rounded clusters of tiny, fragrant, dark purple flowers. Though tender perennials, they are usually grown as annuals. The scent of their flowers is reminiscent of vanilla or, to some noses, cherry pie. The oval, deep green leaves are heavily veined and textured.

Hardiness: Tender.

Blooming Time: Summer to frost.

Height: 8 inches to 3 feet.

Spacing: 1 to 1 ½ feet.

Light: Full sun; needs some afternoon shade in warm climates.

Soil: Well-drained, fertile.

Moisture: Even, regular.

Garden Uses: Grow heliotrope in pots, use it as a bedding plant, or plant it in an old-fashioned cottage or fragrance garden. Heliotrope also makes a wonderfully fragrant cut flower. Cut stems when about half the flowers in the clusters have opened. Make the blooms last longer by cutting a vertical slit in the bottom of the stem, quickly dipping the stem end into boiling water to seal the cuts, and then conditioning the flowers by placing the stems in a container of warm water for several hours.

Comments: Heliotrope is slow to grow from seed, so start it early indoors, 10 to 12 weeks before the last expected frost. Seeds need light to germinate; press them into the soil, but do not cover. Feed them as young seedlings with a half-strength seaweed/fish emulsion dilution. Transplant to the garden with care when all danger of frost has passed; roots do not like to be disturbed. Because you must start the plants so early, many people purchase seedlings from a garden center. Pinch back stem tips of young plants for bushier growth.

To ensure sufficient nutrients for this heavy feeder, make sure the soil is well supplied with compost, or fertilize throughout the growing season with a liquid all-purpose fertilizer or a fish/seaweed product that has been diluted according to the directions on the package. You can also use a half-strength fish/seaweed dilution as a foliar feed if you spray in low-light conditions.

Recommended Cultivars:
- 'Dwarf Marine', slightly over a foot, royal purple flowers
- 'Hybrid Marine', 1 ½ ft.; royal purple; good for cutting
- Marine Lemoine strain, to 2 ft.; purple, good for cutting
- 'Mini Marine', 8–10 in.; deep purple flowers

Deadheading heliotrope

Deadhead heliotrope as the flowers fade, cutting back to the next set of leaves. The plants will send up new flower stalks for much of the summer but eventually exhaust themselves.

Heliotrope makes an excellent companion to the magenta petunias and yellow blackfoot daisies in this garden

IMPATIENS

Impatiens cultivars

'Fiesta Pink Ruffles' double impatiens

Bedding impatiens plants bloom in every imaginable shade of pink, as well as red, orange, lavender, red-violet, and white. Some flowers have a contrasting eye; some are bicolored; and some are full and double. Plants are bushy and mounded with soft oval leaves.

Balsam impatiens is erect and bears its flowers close to the central stem. Many types have double flowers; some are bicolored.

The New Guinea hybrids have larger flowers, mostly in shades of red, rose, lavender, and pink. These are borne on taller plants with longer leaves that are often veined with red and shaded with yellow in the center. Some cultivars have dark red-purple leaves.

Hardiness: Tender.

Blooming Time: All summer until frost.

Height: Bedding impatiens, 4 inches to 1 foot, depending on cultivar; balsam impatiens, 1 to 2 ½ feet, New Guinea impatiens, 1 to 2 feet.

Spacing: 6 inches to 1 foot.

Light: Bedding and balsam impatiens, partial to full shade, tolerates sun with enough moisture; New Guinea impatiens, full sun to partial shade.

Soil: Well-drained, average fertility, lots of organic matter; tolerates a range of soils

Moisture: Needs even, regular moisture.

Garden Uses: Bedding impatiens is widely grown—perhaps too widely—but is still hard to beat for massing in the front of shady beds and borders and under shrubs or for using in pots, window boxes, and hanging baskets. It is easy to grow and among the most versatile of garden plants. Balsam impatiens grows well in the middle of shady or partially shaded gardens, where it can add a colorful vertical accent. New Guinea impatiens grows well in the middle of sunny to partly shady gardens. It is

Saving impatiens seeds

Ripe impatiens seedpods burst when touched, so grasp them firmly and hold a bowl underneath to catch the seeds. The ripe pods appear plump but are still green. They burst open and curl back to release the seeds.

also particularly effective in hanging baskets and other containers.

Comments: Impatiens species can't take cold, so don't plant them out until all danger of frost is past and the weather has warmed in spring.

Impatiens plants don't require deadheading—old flowers will drop off by themselves. The double-flowered type of bedding impatiens tends to drop many of its pretty blossoms shortly after they open, so it's best to water and handle plants with extreme care.

SPACING

1 Impatiens plants are lovely massed under trees or shrubs. Use a ruler to plant at the correct spacing—don't crowd the plants.

2 Plants will fill in quickly to provide a mass of color. Stagger plants so they are equidistant in all directions for best coverage.

'Accent Orange'

Recommended Cultivars:

Bedding types:

- Accent hybrids, 10 in.; 20 colors and combinations
- Mosaic hybrids, 10–12 in.; lilac or rose; splashed white
- Swirl hybrids, 10–12 in.; pastel pink, peach, and coral petals with a darker center and edges
- 'Confection Mix', double flowers; rose, red, orange, pink
- 'Super Elfin', 6 to 10 in.; 20 colors
- 'Tempo', early blooming, 16 colors
- 'Dazzler', 8 inches, 11 colors
- Balsam impatiens:
- 'Blackberry Ice', 2 ft.; double purple flower, white marks
- Tom Thumb series, 1 ft.; double; pink, red, violet, white
- Camellia-flowered series, 2 ½ ft.; double pink or red flowers with white markings.

New Guinea hybrids:

- 'Tango', 1 ft.; bright orange flowers
- 'Spectra Mix', 10 inches to 1 foot, red, rose, coral, scarlet, pink, orchid, and white flowers

Balsam Impatiens

'Light Salmon' New Guinea impatiens

IPOMOEA

Ipomoea tricolor, I. purpurea,
I. nil, **Morning-glory**
I. alba, **Moonflower**
I. batatas, **Sweet potato vine**

These relatives of potatoes and tomatoes are fast-growing twining vines with a multiplicity of uses. The funnel-shaped morning-glory flowers bloom in shades of red, pink, purple, and white, sometimes flushed or striped with a contrasting color. Moonflower vines have large, fragrant white flowers that open in the late afternoon or evening and close with the dawn. The blooms of both moonflowers and morning-glories often have a sheen when they first open. Both plants have large, heart-shaped leaves.

Sweet potato vines have heart-shaped or lobed leaves in attractive colors. The varieties described under "Recommended Cultivars" on the facing page were developed to be purely ornamental. Because the tubers they produce are so tiny, you probably couldn't make these plants do double duty as a food crop anyway; use them only as decorative elements. Cultivars used for food crops tend to have leaves that are far more coarse than those of the cultivars that are used as ornamental plants.

Cypress vine (*I. quamoclit*) has small, brilliant red funnel-shaped flowers with bright white throats. The deep green leaves are so finely divided that they often look threadlike.

Cardinal climber (*I. multifida*) has small scarlet flowers and leaves that are less finely divided. Leaves are a medium green color.

Hardiness: Tender.

Blooming Time: Summer until frost.

Height: Morning-glories, 15 to 20 feet tall; moonflower, 10 to 20 feet tall (or more in warm climates); sweet potato vine, cascading, 5 to 10 feet long; cypress vine, 6 to 12 feet; cardinal climber, 3 to 6 feet.

'Blackie' sweet potato vine

Moonflower

Spacing: 8 inches to 1 foot.

Light: Full sun for the flowering species; sweet potato vines tolerate partial shade.

Soil: Well-drained, average fertility.

Moisture: Moderate to even.

Garden Uses: Morning-glories and moonflowers are lovely on trellises, tripods, obelisks, and fences. Their large leaves make them ideal for

Morning-glories in mixed colors

camouflage, screening, or training on arbors. Or train them up a lamppost or around a mailbox. Moonflowers are heavenly trained around a porch or trellised near a patio or deck where you can sit outdoors on warm summer evenings and enjoy their delightful fragrance. Sweet potato vines are excellent trailing over the edges of containers or hanging baskets. You can also allow them to ramble about the feet of flowers growing in a bed or border, especially in a lush, tropical-looking garden. Try them with colorful coleus and bold cannas and caladiums, along with some hot-colored impatiens plants, for an exuberant tropical effect.

The smaller, more delicate-looking vines of cardinal climber and cypress vine are charming scrambling over shrubs or decorating net trellises or wire mesh fences. They attract hummingbirds, so place them where you can see them from inside the house or a porch.

Comments: Seeds of these plants, especially moonflowers, have hard seed coats. Rub them on sandpaper or nick them with a file before sowing, and/or soak in warm water several hours or overnight before planting. Direct-seed outdoors after all danger of frost is past and the soil is warm. The plants thrive on heat and don't grow well in chilly soil or cool weather. Flowering is affected by temperature; in cool summers your plants won't flower well.

Ornamental sweet potato vines are widely available in garden centers; it's easiest to purchase plants instead of starting your own

Recommended Cultivars:

Morning-glories:

- 'Heavenly Blue', 8 ft.; large sky blue flowers
- 'Early Call Mix', 8–10 ft.; pink, lavender, white flowers
- 'Flying Saucers', to 10 ft.; white flowers; purple streaks
- 'Milky Way', to 15 ft.; white flowers; carmine streaks
- 'Pearly Gates', 8–10 ft.; white flowers
- 'Scarlett O'Hara, 8 ft.; crimson flowers
- 'Star of Yelta', to 6 ft.; deep velvety purple flowers with a rose-pink splash in the center and a white throat
- *I. × imperialis* 'Tie Dye', to 8 ft.; large lavender flowers streaked with darker purple

Moonflower:

- 'Giant White', to 15 ft.; 6-in.-wide fragrant white flowers

Sweet potato vine:

- 'Blackie', deep-purple leaves, angular, pointed lobes
- 'Margarita', heart-shaped leaves of yellow-green
- Cypress vine and Cardinal climber: only as species

Cardinal climber

PREPARING IPOMOEA SEEDS

1 Prepare the hard-coated seeds of this family for planting by scratching them gently against a piece of fine sandpaper.

2 After sanding the seedcoats, soften them further by soaking them in a bowl of lukewarm water for 8 to 24 hours.

Cypress vine

LANTANA

Lantana camara
Yellow sage

Lantanas have wide, domed flower clusters up to 2 inches across. The small individual flowers can be white, yellow, pinkish lavender, or a yellow-red-rusty brown. Flowers of some cultivars change colors as the blooms age: cream changes to pink, pink to lavender, and yellow to orange. In color-changing cultivars, flower clusters may contain three colors at once. The plants are upright, branched, and bushy with toothed, oval leaves. In Zones 10 and 11, the plants are perennial and more shrubby.

Hardiness: Half-hardy.

Blooming Time: All summer.

Height: 4 feet when perennial, 2 feet when annual.

Spacing: 1 to 1 ½ feet.

Light: Full sun.

Soil: Well-drained, average fertility.

Moisture: Average; tolerates some dryness.

Garden Uses: Lantana is an interesting plant for a large container as well as the center or back of the garden. Children find the color-changing flowers magical. Lantana is salt tolerant and useful in seashore gardens. Its flowers are attractive to butterflies.

Comments: Plants grow best in warm weather. All parts of the plants are poisonous if ingested.

Lantana

Recommended Cultivars:

- Mixed hybrids, 1 ½–2 ft.; red-and-yellow, pink-and-yellow, lilac-and-white flowers
- 'Patriot Rainbow', 1 ft.; red-and-yellow flowers.
- Cultivars of L. montevidensis are trailing and grow well in hanging baskets; look for 'White Lightnin'

PROPAGATING YELLOW SAGE

1 Take cuttings from established plants in late summer. Choose stems with at least four nodes. Trim off the blooms and the leaves from the bottom two nodes.

2 Dip each cutting in softwood rooting hormone, and shake off the excess. To avoid contaminating your supply, put the hormone powder in an old bottle or another container.

3 Poke a hole in the planting medium before placing the stem bottom in it. Gently firm the soil so that it is in contact with the stem bottom.

LEUCANTHEMUM

Leucanthemum paludosum (Melampodium paludosum)
Blackfoot daisy, Butter daisy

These bushy, low-growing plants with light green oval leaves are covered with small, yellow or yellowish white daisylike blooms with bright yellow centers. Blackfoot daisies are durable, tough plants.

Hardiness: Half-hardy.

Blooming Time: All summer until frost, sporadically in winter in frost-free climates.

Height: 8 inches to 1 ½ feet.

Spacing: 1 foot.

Light: Full sun.

Soil: Well-drained, average to poor fertility.

Moisture: Average; tolerates drought.

Garden Uses: Plant in the front of the garden or in containers. Blackfoot daisies make the most effective displays when they are planted in masses rather than in small groups. They are excellent companions for annual fountain grass (Pennisetum species), especially the purple-leaved cultivars, and other hot-colored annual flowers, such as scarlet salvia or celosia. In a large mixed container, try them with ornamental sweet potato vines 'Blackie' or 'Margarita', or with spiky dracaena for contrast.

Comments: This plant stands up to hot, humid conditions as well as drought. Start seeds indoors six to eight weeks

Blackfoot daisy seeds

before the last expected frost, and transplant after the danger of frost is past and the soil has warmed. Or direct-seed when the soil is warm. If grown in fertile soils, especially soils rich in nitrogen, the plants will not produce as many flowers. Plants may self-sow.

Blackfoot daisy is easy to maintain. Plants will grow bushy even if you don't pinch them back when young. They are also self-cleaning and need no deadheading.

Recommended Cultivars:
- 'Million Gold', 8–10 in.; golden yellow flowers
- 'Showstar', 10 in.; yellow flowers

'Showstar'

Blackfoot daisy with ornamental grass

LOBELIA

Lobelia erinus
Edging lobelia

Dainty, lipped flowers in clear shades of deep blue, sky blue, red, maroon, pink, and white liberally cover these compact or cascading plants. Leaves are small, elliptical, and dark green. The colored flowers often have a white eye, which adds to their impact.

Hardiness: Half-hardy.

Blooming time: All summer.

Height: 4 to 6 inches.

Spacing: 6 inches.

Light: Full sun to partial shade; appreciates afternoon shade where summers are hot.

Soil: Well-drained, fertile, rich in organic matter.

Moisture: Needs even moisture all summer, but soil must not be soggy.

Garden Uses: These small, delicate-looking plants are lovely in the front of a window box or container. Or use them as edging in a partly shaded garden. The flowers of the blue cultivars positively glow in the shade.

Comments: Lobelia may stop blooming in hot, humid weather, and plants may die back. If flowering slows, shear back the plants—they grow back and resume flowering later in the summer, when nighttime temperatures begin to cool off.

Lobelia

Recommended Cultivars:

- 'Crystal Palace', 5 in.; blue flower, bronze leaves
- 'Mrs. Clibran', 5 in.; dark blue flower with a white eye
- 'Cambridge Blue', 5 in.; light green leaves, blue flowers
- 'Rosamond', 5 in.; wine red flower with a white eye
- 'White Lady', 5 in.; white flowers
- Riviera series, 4 in.; early blooming; deep blue, light blue, blue with white eye, blue-and-white bicolor, white
- 'Cascade Mix', 8 in.; cascading; blue, lavender, red, rose, white, blue with a white eye

PROMOTING A SECOND BLOOM

Cut back lobelia plants if blooming slows in summer or the plants become rangy. Once the weather begins to cool, they will rebloom with vigor.

Lobelia

NICOTIANA

Nicotiana × sanderae
Flowering tobacco

The star-shaped white, red, rose, pink, lavender, and light green flowers have long, tubular throats. They bloom on branched, bushy plants with rather large, narrow-to-oblong leaves of medium green. Plants have an open, rather than a dense, form. The leaves are covered with soft hairs and feel rather sticky to the touch. The flowers of the species form are fragrant at night, but most of the commonly available hybrids have only a faint scent after sundown.

'Lime Green'

Hardiness: Half-hardy.

Blooming Time: All summer.

Height: 1 to 3 feet; the species form grows to 5 feet.

Spacing: 9 inches to 1 foot.

Light: Full sun to partial shade.

Soil: Well-drained, average fertility.

Moisture: Moist; water during spells of hot, dry weather.

Garden Uses: Easy to grow and a prolific bloomer, flowering tobacco is a charming plant to add mass and color in the front or middle ground of a bed or border. It flowers happily in containers too. Place the species form and larger hybrids in the back of the garden.

Comments: A most versatile plant, flowering tobacco performs well in hot sun if it's given enough water; it also blooms nicely in partial to light shade. Sow indoors six to eight weeks before

VOLUNTEER PLANTS

Flowering tobacco self-seeds easily. Thin or transplant the volunteer seedlings as soon as they have their first true leaves.

the last expected frost. Do not cover seeds; they require light to germinate. Transplant to the garden after all danger of frost is past. The leaves and flowers are delicate and easily damaged; handle the plants carefully during transplanting.

If you deadhead regularly, the plants will bloom all summer. When deadheading, cut off the old flower right below its base; new buds will develop on the stem immediately below the old blossom.

Japanese beetles love these plants, so take appropriate measures if these bugs are a problem in your garden.

Recommended Cultivars:

- Domino series, 1 ft.; crimson, red, pink, rose-pink, salmon-pink, purple, white, lime green flowers
- 'Heaven Scent Mix', 2–3 ft.; fragrant at night; red, rose shades, purple, blush white flowers
- Merlin series, to 1 ft.; crimson, purple, peach, white, lime green flowers
- Nicki series, 1 ½–2 ft.; red, pink, white, green flowers

Saving nicotiana seeds

Cut whole seed stalks after the pods turn brown. Don't wait until they are completely dry, or they will drop their seeds on the ground in the first stiff breeze to come along.

PELARGONIUM

Pelargonium x hortorum
Zonal geranium
Pelargonium peltatum
Ivy geranium

Zonal geraniums have round, medium green leaves with scalloped edges, sometimes marked with dark bands (or zones). Large, round clusters of flowers that grow on straight stems bloom in shades of red, pink, red-violet, orange, salmon, and white.

Ivy geraniums have lobed leaves reminiscent of English ivy. The smaller clusters of flowers are airy and graceful and come in shades of red, pink, lavender, and white. The plants have a sprawling or cascading habit no matter where they grow.

Hardiness: Tender.

Blooming Time: All summer until frost.

Height: Zonal, 1 to 3 feet; ivy, trailing 2 to 3 feet.

Spacing: 8 inches to slightly over a foot.

Light: Full sun to partial shade.

Soil: Average to fertile, well-drained.

Moisture: Moderate.

Garden Uses: Zonal geraniums are excellent for bedding, tubs or pots, and the back of a window box. Ivy geraniums are ideal for hanging baskets or window boxes.

Comments: In cool climates, start seeds of zonal geraniums indoors ten to twelve weeks before the last expected frost; transplant out after all danger of frost is past. Take cuttings in late summer to root for indoor bloom in winter. In Zones 10 and 11, zonals will grow outdoors all year.

'L' Elegance', an ivy geranium   *'Mr. Henry Cox', a zonal geranium*

Ivy geraniums are usually propagated from cuttings. Take your own in late summer and overwinter indoors or purchase plants in spring.

Recommended Cultivars: Zonals:

- Elite series, 10 in.; early blooming; zoned leaves; flowers are rose-pink, salmon-orange, red shades, white
- Multibloom series, 8–10 in.; red, scarlet, rose, pink, salmon, lavender, white flowers
- Orbit series, 1 ft.; zoned leaves; compact plants; red, scarlet, pink, lavender-pink, violet, salmon flowers

Ivy geraniums:

- 'Summer Showers Mixed', 2–3 ft.; red, burgundy, pink, rose, lavender, white flowers

'Kim', a zonal geranium

PROPAGATING GERANIUMS

Take cuttings in late summer to root and grow as houseplants over the winter. In late winter, take cuttings again to grow for the summer garden.

PETUNIA

Petunia x hybrida

Fragrant, funnel-shaped flowers in many shades of red, purple, pink, blue, white, and pale yellow cover petunia plants. Some are bicolored and some are striped or edged with white (picotees). Flowers are single or double, smooth or ruffled. Multiflora types bear smaller, mostly single flowers, while grandiflora types have larger, often double flowers. Wave types spread or cascade farther than others. The leaves are soft, hairy, and a bit sticky.

Hardiness: Half-hardy.

Blooming Time: All summer if deadheaded regularly.

Height: 8 inches to slightly over a foot for upright types.

Spacing: 10 inches to 1 foot.

Light: Full sun to partial shade.

Soil: Average, well-drained; tolerates a range of soils.

Moisure: Average to moist.

Garden Uses: Plant petunias in the front of beds and borders, or in pots or window boxes. Spreading types, particularly the Wave series, can be used for ground covers.

Comments: Sow indoors about 10 weeks before the last expected frost. Do not cover the seeds; they need light to germinate. Seedlings will be tiny. Transplant them to cell packs or peat pots after they have several sets of leaves. If you seeded them in a soilless mix, water with a seaweed/fish dilution to keep them healthy.

Transplant out when danger of frost is past. Petunias tend to look ratty by midsummer; cutting back the lanky stems encourages a neater habit and renewed bloom. Heavy rain and wind may damage plants, especially grandiflora types.

Recommended Cultivars:

Multifloras:

- Fantasy series, 10 in.; called "milliflora" in the nursery trade; the earliest to bloom; small red, pink, blue, salmon, white flowers

- Celebrity series, 9–12 in.; red shade and pink shade flowers, also salmon, peach, lilac, blue, white flowers, all with white throats

- Merlin series, 10 in.; early blooming; reds, salmon, blue, white, several picotees

- Primetime series, 11 in.; many colors

Multiflora petunia

- Wave series, spreading plants 4–6 in. high and 2–4 ft. wide; plum, coral, rose-pink flowers

- 'Heavenly Lavender', 1 ft.; deep lavender flowers

- 'Polo Mixed', 10 in.; weather-resistant flowers; red, pink, purple, white, some striped or with deeper colored veins

Grandifloras:

- 'Blue Danube', 1 ft.; lavender flowers with blue veins

- Daddy series, about 1 ft.; flowers are veined with dark, contrasting colors in shades of pink, orchid, blue

- 'Double Delight Mixed', 1 ft.; double red, pink, purple, white, bicolored flowers

- 'Double Cascade', about 1 ft.; double pink and burgundy flowers resembling carnations

- Falcon series, shades of red, pink, salmon, blue, white, and plum, some with colorful veins

Cutting back petunias

Cut back elongated, bare stems in midsummer, trimming to just above a node or pair of leaves. Plants will respond by developing new, more tidy, growth.

Grandiflora petunia

PORTULACA

Portulaca grandiflora
Rose moss

Silky, ruffly diaphanous blossoms, single or double, characterize rose mosses. Flowers bloom in many warm shades—red, rose, magenta, pink, salmon, gold, yellow, and white. The plants are low and creeping, with fleshy, needlelike foliage.

Hardiness: Tender.

Blooming Time: All summer into autumn.

Height: The trailing stems grow to 10 inches long, but plants are usually no more than 6 inches tall.

Spacing: 8 to 10 inches.

Light: Full sun.

Soil: Well-drained, preferably sandy; tolerates poor, dry soil.

Moisture: Prefers soil on the dry side; drought tolerant.

Garden Uses: Rose moss is an excellent small plant for hot, dry conditions. The brilliantly colored flowers are a cheerful edging along paths and pavements and in the front of sunny beds and borders. It's also a terrific plant for containers and hanging baskets. Some newer hybrids that are especially well suited to hanging baskets have smaller flowers and spoon-shaped leaves streaked with white and green. Try planting rose moss in pockets of soil in stone walls, or use them to add a bright festive touch in front of or along the top of a wall. Portulacas make a wonderful carpet for an area of poor, somewhat dry soil.

Rose moss

Comments: Sow indoors four to six weeks before the last frost; transplant when all danger of frost is past. Don't fertilize because high nutrient levels suppress flowering.

The plants may self-sow; dig up unwanted volunteers. Blossoms close at dark and reopen in the morning.

Recommended Cultivars:

- 'Calypso Mixed', 5 in.; double flowers in warm colors
- Sundial hybrids, 5–6 in.; large double flowers in red, scarlet, pink, gold, white, peach

SITING ROSE MOSS

Rose moss can thrive in areas that are adjacent to hot pavement, such as this sidewalk cutout. The plants don't require much moisture or nutrients, so they also make a good under-story plant for limbed-up trees.

Rose moss seeds next to a dime

SALVIA

Salvia coccinea, Salvia farinacea, **Mealycup sage**
Salvia splendens, **Scarlet sage**

Annual salvia species vary tremendously from one another. But even though they display a wide range of colors and flower types, all of them are easy to grow and long blooming. Salvia coccinea has loose spikes of tubular flowers of red, coral, or white. Mealycup sage bears spikes of tiny, tubular flowers of rich violet-blue or grayish white on straight, slender stems. Cultivars of scarlet sage have smaller spikes of somewhat larger tubular blossoms of brilliant scarlet or, less commonly, purple, pink, or creamy white. The upright, branched to bushy plants have oval to lance-shaped leaves.

Hardiness: Half-hardy

Blooming Time: All summer to frost.

Height: 10 inches to 3 feet, depending on variety.

Spacing: 8 inches to 1 ½ feet; don't crowd the plants because they become bushier as they mature.

Light: Full sun to partial shade; provide some afternoon shade in hot climates.

Soil: Well-drained, average fertility.

Moisture: Average to moist; salvias don't grow well in arid climates. Scarlet sage needs more even moisture than mealycup sage.

Garden Uses: Annual salvias are rewarding; they send up new flower spikes all summer long and need deadheading much less frequently than many other flowers. The plants provide a welcome vertical accent in the front or middle of beds and borders or in containers. The flowers can also be cut for fresh arrangements or dried.

Mealycup sage is perennial in Zones 8 and warmer. It is among the most rewarding of garden flowers—adapting to a great range of soils and growing conditions, blooming lavishly all season, and holding its flowers for a long time. The plants branch naturally and need no pinching when they are young to make them full and bushy. The flowers are excellent for cutting. Blue cultivars dry to a lovely soft shade of blue that can add bulk and color to lavender flowers in a potpourri.

To use salvias in fresh arrangements, cut flowers when the lowest blooms on the spike have opened and the higher blossoms are still closed. Place the stems in a container of warm water for several hours to condition the flowers. Before arranging them, remove any leaves that would be underwater in the vase. The narrow flower spikes add vertical interest to bouquets and arrangements.

The flowers can be air-dried, but to preserve the most color when drying salvias, lay them horizontally in a container of silica gel, and carefully sprinkle or brush more desiccant over and around the flowers until they are completely covered.

The bright red of scarlet sage can be difficult to combine with flowers in cool hues, but surrounding it with white flowers and deep green foliage makes for an effective display. The newer, softer pink and purple shades are easier to work with. In Zones 9 and warmer, plant for spring or fall bloom.

Comments: Sow mealycup sage indoors about 10 weeks before the last expected frost and scarlet sage six to eight weeks before then. Do not cover the seeds; salvias need light to germinate. They also require warm temperatures; don't plant them outdoors until all danger of frost is past in spring. With occasional deadheading, the plants will keep blooming all summer long, right up until frost strikes them.

Recommended Cultivars:

S. coccinea

- 'Lady in Red', 2 ft.; bright red flowers
- 'Coral Nymph', 2 ft.; coral-and-white bicolored flowers
- 'Snow Nymph', 2 ft.; white flowers

S. farinacea

- 'White Porcelain', 1 ½ ft.; white flowers
- 'Victoria', 1 ½ ft.; violet-blue; long-blooming

S. splendens

- 'Flare', 1 ½ ft.; bright red flowers
- 'Carabiniere', slightly over 1 ft.; blood-red flowers
- Sizzler series, 1–1 ½ ft.; red, burgundy, rose, pink, purple, plum, lavender, salmon, white flowers

Scarlet sage

Mealycup sage

SENECIO

Senecio cineraria
Dusty miller

These upright, branched bushy plants are grown for their velvety, deeply cut, silver-white foliage. The leaves have a lacy, frilly look.

Hardiness: Tender.

Height: 8 inches to 2 feet, depending on variety.

Spacing: 10 inches to 1 foot.

Light: Full sun.

Soil: Very well drained, average fertility.

Moisture: Average to rather dry.

Garden Uses: The silver-leaved dusty millers are valuable accents for flower gardens and containers; they are especially pretty with pink and blue flowers. Their cool foliage can be used to tone down beds of hot-colored flowers or add shimmer to a garden of white flowers.

Comments: Start seeds indoors in late winter (February) and plant outdoors when all danger of frost has passed. Or purchase plants; they are widely available. The plants are actually tender perennials and may overwinter in Zones 8 to 11. Plants may send up clusters of small, not very ornamental ivory or yellow flowers at the tips of upright stems; for appearance's sake, pinch out the flower stems if they appear.

Like most silver-leaved plants, dusty miller tolerates a fair degree of drought and suffers in soils that are continuously wet. Pinch the plants when they are young to encourage bushy, compact growth.

In addition to *Senecio* cultivars, some other plants are sold under the name of dusty miller. Two particularly

'Silverdust'

nice ones are cultivars of *Chrysanthemum* (or *Tanacetum*) *ptarmiciflorum*: 'Silver Lace', to about 10 inches high with finely dissected, lacy-looking leaves, and 'Silver Feather', to 12 inches high, also with finely cut, feathery leaves.

Recommended Cultivars:
- 'Silverdust', 8 in.
- 'Cirrus', 8–10 in.; larger, whiter leaves; good tolerance to rain and light frost

PINCHING SENECIO

Promote bushiness by pinching back stem tips as the plants grow.

Removing flowers

Remove the flower stalks from dusty miller plants as soon as they form rather than after they bloom.

TAGETES

Tagetes erecta, **African or American marigold**
Tagetes patula, **French marigold**
Tagetes tenuifolia, **Signet marigold**

Marigolds are loved for their freely blooming, sunny flowers of yellow or orange. African marigolds are up-right plants with flowers that are usually 2 to 4 inches across. The so-called "white" cultivars have flowers that are really a lovely pale yellow. French marigolds are small, bushy plants with small flowers of yellow, orange, or deep mahogany red. Signet marigolds are smaller still, with masses of diminutive flowers of yellow or orange and somewhat lemon-scented foliage; the blossoms are edible. All marigolds have divided, ferny leaves composed of narrow leaflets.

African marigold

French marigold

Signet marigold

Hardiness: Half-hardy.

Blooming Time: All summer until frost if deadheaded regularly.

Height: African, 1 to 2 ½ feet; French, 6 inches to 1 ½ feet; signets, 6 inches to 1 foot.

Spacing: African, 1 to 2 feet; French and signet, 6 inches to 1 foot.

Light: Full sun.

Soil: Well-drained, average to good fertility.

Moisture: Average.

Garden Uses: All are good additions to beds, borders, and cottage gardens; they also grow well in pots, tubs, and window boxes. Place African marigolds in the middle of the garden, and use the smaller types for edging. Taller cultivars of African and French marigolds make good cut flowers, too.

Comments: Marigolds are tender annuals and thrive in hot weather. Start seeds indoors six to eight weeks before the last expected frost; don't plant outdoors until all danger of frost is past. In Zones 9 and warmer, direct-seed in early spring.

Recommended Cultivars:
African:
- Antigua series, 1–1 ½ ft.; orange, yellow flowers
- Discovery series, 10 in.; yellow, orange flowers
- Excel series, slightly over 1 ft.; yellow, orange flowers
- Inca series, 1–1 ½ ft.; yellow, gold, bright orange flowers
- 'Jubilee', 1 ½–2 ft.; shades of yellow, orange flowers

DEADHEADING MARIGOLDS

Deadhead flowers as soon as they fade, and plants will reward you with flowers through the season.

- Lady series, 1 ½ ft.; lemon yellow, gold, orange flowers
- 'Snowdrift', to 2 ft.; ivory to pale yellow flowers
- 'French Vanilla', 2 ft.; ivory-white flowers

French:
- Bonanza series, 8 in.; yellow/gold bicolors, red shades
- Disco series, 1 ft.; single flowers; red, orange, yellow
- Janie series, 8 in.; orange, yellow bicolors with red
- Zenith series, 1 ft.; yellow, orange, orange-and-red
- 'Mr Majestic', 1 ft.; red-striped yellow flowers look like pinwheels

Signet:
- 'Starfire Mix', 1 ft. or slightly over; yellow, orange, red
- 'Tangerine Gem', small orange flowers
- 'Lemon Gem', small yellow flowers

TITHONIA

Tithonia rotundifolia
Mexican sunflower

These big, branching plants bear large, hot-colored, daisy-shaped blooms in shades of bright red-orange and brilliant yellow with yellow centers. The flowers look similar to zinnias or single-petaled dahlias. The large, coarse deep green leaves are oblong and feel velvety. These are tender perennials but gardeners in most locations grow them as annuals.

Mexican sunflower

Hardiness: Tender.

Blooming Time: All summer until frost, peaks in late summer.

Height: 2 ½ to 6 feet, depending on cultivar.

Spacing: 2 to 3 feet.

Light: Full sun.

SAVING MEXICAN SUNFLOWER SEEDS

Wait until the petals drop and the flower heads dry to cut for seed-saving. Allow the seeds to dry several more weeks before packing for winter storage.

Soil: Well-drained, average to poor fertility.

Moisture: Moderate to somewhat dry; some drought tolerance.

Garden Uses: Plant Mexican sunflowers in the back of the garden or use them for screening or even a temporary hedge. The flowers attract butterflies and hummingbirds. Plants tolerate high heat, humidity, and drought. The flowers are good for cutting and are long lasting in the vase. Cut flowers when they are almost fully open and the centers are still tight. Morning or early evening is the best time to cut. Before arranging in a vase, pass the cut ends of the brittle, hollow stems over a candle flame until the end of the stem has calloused over, or dip them in boiling water for just a second or two to seal them. Unsealed stems will bleed and foul the water. After sealing, stand the stems in a container of warm water almost to the base of the flowers for several hours before arranging them.

Comments: Direct-sow in spring, when frost danger is past, or sow indoor six to eight weeks earlier and plant out after the last frost date. Stake plants growing in windy locations; the tall stems may snap or blow over if buffeted by strong winds on a regular basis.

Recommended Cultivars:
- 'Aztec Sun', 4 ft.; yellow-orange flowers
- 'Fiesta Del Sol', 2 ft.; bright orange flowers
- 'Goldfinger', 2 ½ ft.; red-orange flowers
- 'Torch', 6 ft.; scarlet-orange flowers

Staking

Stake Mexican sunflower plants if you live in a windy area. Without staking, the stems are likely to topple over onto the ground when the plants mature.

TORENIA

Torenia fournieri
Wishbone flower

Wishbone flowers get their name from paired stamens inside the throat that resemble a wishbone. The enchanting tubular flowers are two shades of violet-blue and purple, or violet and white, with a yellow splash in the throat. There are also cultivars with white or rosy to clear pink flowers. The petals are velvety, like those of pansies. The small, upright, bushy plants have more or less oval leaves.

Hardiness: Tender.

Blooming Time: Midsummer to frost.

Height: 10 inches to 1 foot.

Spacing: 6 to 8 inches.

Light: Partial to light shade.

Soil: Well-drained, average to good fertility.

Moisture: Keep evenly moist but not soggy; wishbone flowers don't tolerate dry soil.

Garden Uses: These pretty little plants deserve to be known better. They are lovely for edging shady beds and borders or massing on a shady slope or under a tree with an open, high canopy. Because this plant flowers so prolifically and is so eye-catching, it makes a large impact when massed. Wishbone flowers also grow well in pots and hanging baskets in partly shaded locations. They make a nice change from, or companion to, impatiens because they thrive in the same sort of conditions.

The flowers can also be used for fresh-cut blooms, serving as fillers or accents in arrangements. Cut stems that

TRANSPLANTING

Transplant wishbone flowers after the frost-free date.

have several just-opened blossoms in the morning or early evening. Cut one or two vertical slits up into the cut end of each stem; then condition them by standing the stems in a container of tepid water nearly to the base of the lowest blooms. Leave them in the water for several hours before arranging the flowers. Buds will continue to open after the flowers are arranged and in the vase.

Comments: Don't plant wishbone flowers in the garden or set potted plants outside until all danger of frost is past in spring. Sow seeds indoors 10 to 12 weeks earlier. Press seeds lightly into moist soil, but do not cover them.

The plants do not tolerate cold but thrive on heat, as long as they are not allowed to dry out.

Recommended Cultivar:
• 'Clown Mix', 8–10 in.; violet, rose-pink, white flowers

Wishbone flower

Starting seeds
Use plastic film over the flats to keep the soil medium moist.

VIOLA

Viola x wittrockiana
Pansy

A favorite for spring planting, pansies are available—with or without the distinctive clown-face markings—in an extensive range of colors, including shades of purple, blue, yellow, orange, red, pink, white, and deep blue-black. The compact plants are found in practically every garden center where bedding plants are sold in early spring and also, increasingly, in fall.

Blooming Time: Spring into summer, or autumn; winter to early spring in warm climates.

Height: 5 to 10 inches.

Spacing: 6 to 8 inches.

Light: Full sun to partial shade.

Soil: Well-drained, fertile, rich in organic matter.

Moisture: Abundant, even.

Garden Uses: Use pansies as edging, in the front of beds and borders, as companions to spring bulbs, and in pots and window boxes. The flowers can be used in small arrangements by themselves or in arrangements with other flowers; they last up to about five days in the vase. Keeping the arrangement in a cool room will maximize the life of the flowers. Cut flowers when nearly open, in the morning or early evening. Soak the flowers, stems and all, in cold water for an hour or so to firm them up so they don't go limp; then stand the stems upright in a container of cool water nearly to the base of the flowers for several hours before arranging them.

Pansies are edible and make charming additions to salads. You can candy them by painting the petals with beaten egg white and dusting them with superfine granulated sugar. Let the flowers dry; then store them, if necessary, between sheets of wax paper in a covered container. Use the candied blossoms to decorate baked goods and desserts.

Pansies grow best in cool weather. Regular deadheading will prolong their bloom, but hot weather will shut down the plants no matter what you do. Pull them up, and replant the area with hot-weather annuals.

'Accord Clear Primrose'

Recommended Cultivars:

- 'Antique Shades', 6 in.; pastel pink, rose, apricot, yellow, cream flowers
- 'Crystal Bowl Mixed', 6–8 in.; scarlet, rose, orange, yellow, white, blue shades
- Swiss Giant hybrids, red, burgundy, rose, orange, bronze, yellow, blue, white, violet flowers
- 'Fall Colors', scarlet, orange, yellow, bronze flowers
- 'Jolly Joker', orange-and-purple bicolored blooms
- Maxim series, 6 in.; mahogany, red, orange, pink, violet, bicolored flowers with white, all with a contrasting blotch, or "face"

'Universal True Blue'

Comments: Sow indoors 12 weeks before the last expected heavy frost. Set out plants two weeks before the last expected frost. Warm-climate gardeners can sow in late summer or fall for late winter flowers. Plants will overwinter in a cold frame as far north as Zone 5.

Saving pansy seeds

Collect the seeds before they drop to the ground. Try to pick the pods just before they split. If that will be impossible, tie row cover material around nearly ripe pods to catch the falling seeds.

ZINNIA

Zinnia angustifolia,
Narrow-leaved zinnia
Zinnia elegans,
Common zinnia

Common garden zinnias (Z. elegans) come in a range of sizes. Flowers are single or double, and the palette contains many shades of red, orange, pink, and yellow, along with creamy whites and an unusual light green. Narrow-leaved zinnia is a charming smaller plant with small, single flowers.

Zinnia elegans

Zinnia angustifolia

Blooming Time: Summer.

Height: Narrow-leaved, to 1 foot, sprawling; Common, 6 inches to 3 feet.

Spacing: Narrow-leaved, 6 inches to 1 foot; Common, 6 inches to slightly over 1 foot.

Light: Full sun; tolerates a bit of shade in warm climates.

Soil: Well-drained, average fertility; common zinnias tolerate somewhat richer soils.

Moisture: Average; tolerates some dryness.

Garden Uses: Zinnias are dependable plants for beds and borders; plant them in the front or middle of the garden according to their size. There are tall, large-flowered common zinnias for the back of the garden, dwarf sizes for the front of the garden, and medium-size plants to use in between. Narrow-leaved zinnia is good for edging or the front of window boxes and containers. Both are delightful in cottage gardens. Garden zinnias make good cut flowers, too.

Comments: Zinnias thrive in hot weather. Sow seeds outdoors after all danger of frost is past in spring. In short-season areas, start indoors six weeks before the last expected frost and transplant to the garden when the weather has settled. Seedlings don't like root disturbance; plant in peat pots and transplant carefully.

In cool, humid conditions, zinnias are often troubled by powdery mildew and leaf spots, especially late in the season. Water early in the day so that leaves dry before nightfall, and pick off affected leaves. Cultivars with narrow leaves are often more resistant to these diseases than common zinnias.

Recommended Cultivars:

Z. angustifolia:

- 'Crystal White', 8 in.; white flowers
- 'Star Gold', 8–12 in.; yellow

- 'Star Orange', 8–12 in.; orange flowers
- 'Star White' (or 'White Star'), 8–12 in.; white flowers
- Pinwheel series, 1 ft.; single; reds, orange, yellow, white

Z. elegans:

- 'Big Red', 3 ft.; rich red flowers
- Border Beauty series, 1 ½–2 ft.; reds, orange, yellow
- 'Candy Stripe', 2 ft.; white splashed with red, rose-pink
- 'Envy', 1 ½–2 ft.; lime green flowers
- Peter Pan series, 1 ft.; scarlet, orange, pink, gold, cream
- Pulcino series, 1–1 ½ ft.; red shades, rose, pink, orange, salmon, gold flowers
- Ruffled hybrids, 2 ½ ft.; ruffled petals colored cherry red, pink, yellow

CUTTING ZINNIAS

Cutting zinnias for arrangements and deadheading excess flowers will keep plants blooming well.

Zinnias are ideal companions for the tansy, goldenrod, mums, asters, and nasturtiums that make up this arrangement.

Zone maps

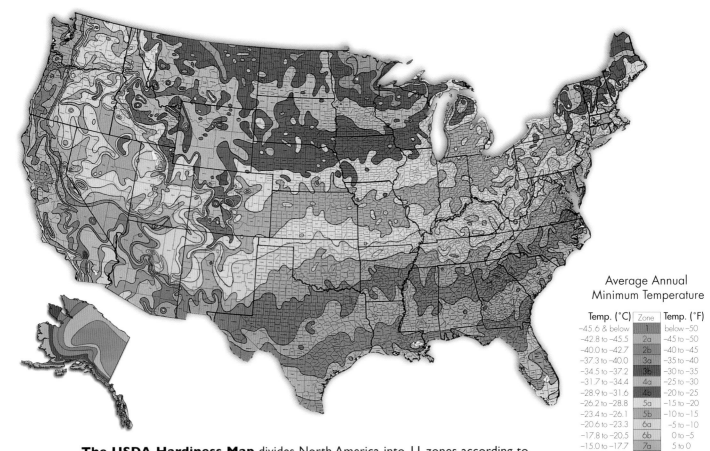

Average Annual Minimum Temperature

Temp. (°C)	Zone	Temp. (°F)
−45.6 & below	1	below −50
−42.8 to −45.5	2a	−45 to −50
−40.0 to −42.7	2b	−40 to −45
−37.3 to −40.0	3a	−35 to −40
−34.5 to −37.2	3b	−30 to −35
−31.7 to −34.4	4a	−25 to −30
−28.9 to −31.6	4b	−20 to −25
−26.2 to −28.8	5a	−15 to −20
−23.4 to −26.1	5b	−10 to −15
−20.6 to −23.3	6a	−5 to −10
−17.8 to −20.5	6b	0 to −5
−15.0 to −17.7	7a	5 to 0
−12.3 to −15.0	7b	10 to 5
−9.5 to −12.2	8a	15 to 10
−6.7 to −9.4	8b	20 to 15
−3.9 to −6.6	9a	25 to 20
−1.2 to −3.6	9b	30 to 25
1.6 to −1.1	10a	35 to 30
4.4 to 1.7	10b	40 to 35
4.5 & above	11	40 & above

The USDA Hardiness Map divides North America into 11 zones according to average minimum winter temperatures. Hardiness zones are used to identify regions to which plants are suited based on their cold tolerance, which is what "hardiness" means. Many factors, such as elevation and moisture level, come into play when determining whether a plant is suitable for your region. Local climates may vary from what is shown on this map. Contact your local Cooperative Extension Service for recommendations for your area.

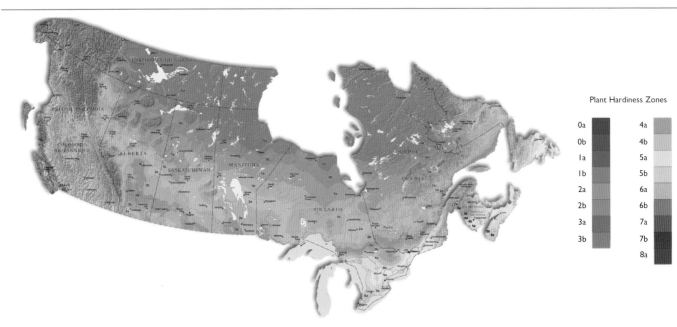

Plant Hardiness Zones

0a	4a
0b	4b
1a	5a
1b	5b
2a	6a
2b	6b
3a	7a
3b	7b
	8a

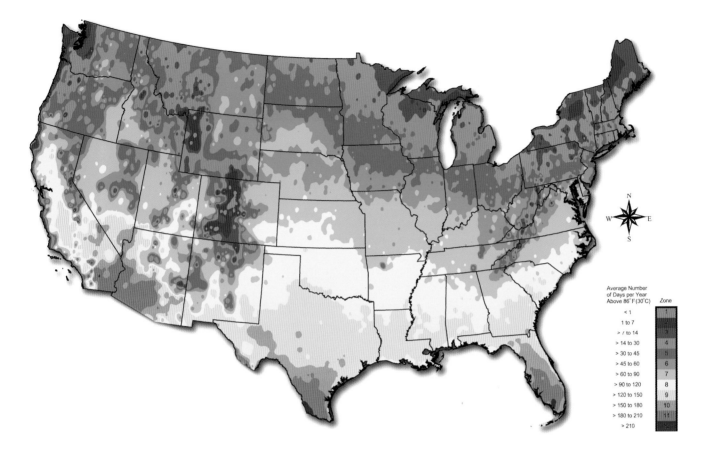

Average Number of Days per Year Above 86°F (30°C)	Zone
< 1	1
1 to 7	2
> 7 to 14	3
> 14 to 30	4
> 30 to 45	5
> 45 to 60	6
> 60 to 90	7
> 90 to 120	8
> 120 to 150	9
> 150 to 180	10
> 180 to 210	11
> 210	12

The American Horticultural Society Heat-Zone Map divides the United States into 12 zones based on the average annual number of days a region's temperatures climb above 86°F (30°C), the temperature at which the cellular proteins of plants begin to experience injury. Introduced in 1998, the AHS Heat-Zone Map holds significance, especially for gardeners in southern and transitional zones. Nurseries, growers, and other plant sources will gradually begin listing both cold hardiness and heat tolerance zones for plants, including grass plants. Using the USDA Plant Hardiness map, which can help determine a plant's cold tolerance, and the AHS Heat-Zone Map, gardeners will be able to safely choose plants that tolerate their region's lowest and highest temperatures.

Canada's Plant Hardiness Zone Map outlines the different zones in Canada where various types of trees, shrubs, and flowers will most likely survive. It is based on the average climatic conditions of each area. The hardiness map is divided into nine major zones: the harshest is 0 and the mildest is 8. Relatively few plants are suited to zone 0. Subzones (e.g., 4a or 4b, 5a or 5b) are also noted in the map legend. These subzones are most familiar to Canadian gardeners. Some significant local factors, such as micro-topography, amount of shelter, and subtle local variations in snow cover, are too small to be captured on the map. Year-to-year variations in weather and gardening techniques can also have a significant impact on plant survival in any particular location.

Glossary

Acid soil A soil that tests lower than 7.0 on the pH scale.

Alkaline soil A soil that tests higher than 7.0 on the pH scale.

Amendments Organic or inorganic materials that improve soil structure, drainage, and nutrient-holding capacity. Some add nutrients.

Annual A plant that completes its entire life cycle in one growing season.

Axil The upper angle between a main stem and its branches or leaf petioles.

Basal plate The flat structure at the bottom of a bulb from which the roots grow.

Biennial A plant that completes its life-cycle in two years. Most biennials form a rosette of leaves the first year and a flower stalk the second.

Bract A modified leaf that sometimes looks like a flower petal.

Bud An embryonic flower, leaf, or stem. Buds form on stems or plant crowns.

Bulb A fleshy underground structure that stores nutrients during a plant's annual dormant period. A true bulb is a modified flower bud or shoot enclosed in scales, or enlarged overlapping modified leaves. Other types of underground storage structures—tubers, tuberous roots, corms, and rhizomes—are often referred to as bulbs.

Bulb pan A a wide shallow pan or pot used for forcing spring bulbs.

Calyx The protective modified leaves, or sepals, that surround the base of a flower.

Compound leaf A leaf that is divided into two or more distinct leaflets.

Corm The underground, swollen base of a stem from which new shoots and roots can grow. Crocuses grow from corms.

Corolla The group of petals that form a flower.

Corona The central cup- or tube-shaped part of a flower such as a daffodil.

Cotyledon The first leaf or set of leaves that a plant grows; these are also called seed leaves.

Crown The part of the plant where roots and stem meet, generally just below or at the soil line.

Cultivar Short for cultivated variety. Rather than occurring naturally in the wild, cultivars are developed. Cultivar names are enclosed in single quotes.

Cutting A piece of stem or root that is removed from a plant and used to propagate a new plant.

Deadheading Removing flowers after they have faded. Some plants prolong their bloom time when deadheaded.

Disbudding Removing some flower buds to promote larger flowers from remaining buds.

Disk flowers The small flowers in the center of a composite flower head such as a sunflower or daisy.

Division A propagation method that separates a plant into two or more pieces, each with at least one bud and some roots.

Foliar feeding To spray a plant's leaves with a fertilizer containing immediately available nutrients.

Forcing Causing a plant to flower indoors ahead of its natural blooming time.

Full shade Refers to a site that receives no direct sunlight.

Full sun Refers to a site that receives six or more hours a day of direct sunlight.

Genus (plural: genera) A closely related group of species that share similar characteristics. Genus names are italicized and capitalized.

Harden off To gradually acclimate a seedling started indoors to the harsher outdoor environment.

Hardiness A plant's ability to survive the climate in an area without protection from winter cold or summer heat, often described in relation to official Hardiness Zones.

Hardy annual An annual that can tolerate cool temperatures. Some hardy annuals tolerate freezing temperatures for short periods of time.

Herbaceous Plants whose stems and leaves die back to the ground each winter are herbaceous rather than woody.

Humus A material derived from the almost completely decomposed remains of organic matter. Highly complex in make-up, humus buffers soil acidity and alkalinity, holds water and nutrients, improves soil aggregation and structure, and contains many compounds that enhance plant growth.

Hybrid A plant resulting from cross breeding parent plants that belong to different varieties or cultivars, species, or sometimes even genera. Hybrids can be indicated by a times sign (×) between the genus and species name or the designation F1 or F2.

Inflorescence Any sort of flower cluster on a common stem. Sometimes used to refer to a single flower.

Invasive A plant that spreads easily and thus "invades" adjacent areas.

Leaflet One of the divisions on a compound leaf.

Microclimate Conditions of sun, shade, exposure, wind, drainage, and other factors at a particular site.

Mulch A covering on the soil. Mulches can be inorganic, as in plastic films, or organic, as in straw, chipped leaves, or shredded bark.

Node The point along a stem from which a leaf or roots emerge.

Offset A new plant that forms vegetatively; it usually grows at the base of the parent plant.

Perennial A plant that normally lives for three or more years.

Pesticide A substance that kills insect pests. The term is also used to describe other agricultural toxins, including fungicides and herbicides.

Petiole The stem of a leaf.

pH A measure of acidity or alkalinity. The pH scale runs from 0 to 14, where 7 represents neutral, numbers higher than 7 represent alkalinity and those lower than 7 represent acidity.

Plant habit The form a plant naturally takes as it grows, such as spreading, columnar, or rounded.

Propagate To create more plants. Plants also reproduce, or propagate, themselves.

Ray flowers The flowers surrounding the central disk in a composite flower.

Rhizome A creeping, often enlarged, stem that lies at or just under the soil surface. Both shoots and roots can form at nodes along the rhizome.

Rosette A low-growing, generally circular cluster of leaves that arises from a plant's crown.

Runner A low-growing stem that arises from the crown and runs along the ground. Runners can root at every node.

Seed leaf The first leaf or set of leaves produced by the embryo of a plant during its germination period. Also called a cotyledon.

Self-cleaning A term used to describe a plant that does not require deadheading. Spent flowers drop off by themselves and the plant continues to make new blooms.

Species A group of plants that shares many characteristics and can interbreed freely. The species name follows the genus name, is italicized, and is not capitalized.

Succulent Fleshy, water-filled plant tissues. Plants with tissues like these are often referred to as a succulent.

Tender perennial A plant that is perennial in frost-free environments but dies when exposed to freezing temperatures.

True leaf The second and subsequent leaves or sets of leaves that a plant produces. The first leaf or set of leaves are seed leaves, or cotyledons. True leaves have the distinctive shape of the leaves of the mature plant.

Tuber A swollen stem that grows underground. Both roots and shoots grow from tubers.

Tuberous roots Enlarged roots that have growth buds at the crown (the area where the plant's roots meet the stems).

Variegated Foliage that is marked, striped, or blotched with a color other than the basic green of the leaf.

Whorl Leaves or petals growing in a circular cluster around a stem.

Index

Photo Credits

page 1: Dennis Frates/Positive Images **page 3:** *from top down* David Cavagnaro; David Cavagnaro; Derek Fell; Rob Cardillo **page 4** *all* David Cavagnaro **page 5** *top* Neil Soderstrom; *bottom* Jerry Pavia **page 6:** *clockwise from top left* David Cavagnaro; David Cavagnaro; The Garden Picture Library; David Cavagnaro; Charles Mann **page 7:** *top right* Sonnim/Shutterstock; *bottom left* John Glover; *bottom right* Jerry Howard **page 8:** *left and top* David Cavagnaro; *right* Jerry Pavia **page 9:** *left* Jane Legate/Garden Picture Library; *right* John Glover **page 10:** *all* Neil Soderstrom **page 11:** *left* Neil Soderstrom; *middle* David Cavagnaro; *right* Neil Soderstrom **page 12:** *all* David Cavagnaro **page 13:** *all* David Cavagnaro **page 14:** *top middle* John Glover; *bottom* Friedrich Strauss/The Garden Picture Library **page 15:** *all* David Cavagnaro **page 16:** *top left* Catriona Tudor Erler; *top right* David Cavagnaro; *bottom right* The Garden Picture Library; *bottom left* Derek Fell **page 17:** *top* Crandall & Crandall; *bottom* Neil Soderstrom **page 18:** *left* John Glover; *right* Positive Images **page 19:** *left* Derek Fell; *right* Jerry Pavia **page 20:** *all* Charles Mann **page 21:** Rosalind Creasy **page 22:** John Glover **page 23:** Jerry Pavia **page 24:** *all* John Glover **page 25:** *left* David Cavagnaro; *top right* John Glover; *bottom right* The Garden Picture Library **page 26:** John Glover **page 27:** *left* Derek Fell; *right* David Cavagnaro **page 28:** *left* Neil Soderstrom; *top right* Walter Chandoha; *bottom right* David Cavagnaro **page 29:** *all* Neil Soderstrom **page 30:** *all* Neil Soderstrom **page 31:** *all* Neil Soderstrom **page 32:** *top* Charles Mann; *bottom* David Cavagnaro **page 33:** *top* David Cavagnaro; *bottom* Michael Thompson **page 34:** *all* David Cavagnaro **page 35:** Neil Soderstrom **page 36:** *top* Jerry Howard; *bottom* Neil Soderstrom **page 37:** Neil Soderstrom **page 38:** *top* David Cavagnaro; *bottom* Photo Researchers **page 39:** *top left* Photo Researchers; *top right* Nigel Cattlin; *bottom right* Photo Researchers **page 40:** *top left* Neil Soderstrom; *bottom left and right* The Garden Picture Library **page 41:** Jerry Howard **page 42:** *all* David Cavagnaro **page 43:** Charles Mann **page 44:** *top left* David Cavagnaro; *top right* Photos Horticultural; *bottom right* Rob Cardillo; *bottom left* Derek Fell **page 45:** Rosalind Creasy **page 47:** Garden Picture Library **page 48:** *all* Neil Soderstrom **page 49:** *all* Derek Fell **page 52:** *all* David Cavagnaro **page 53:** *top right* Neil Soderstrom; *bottom right* David Cavagnaro; *bottom left* Neil Soderstrom **page 54:** *top right* David Cavagnaro; *bottom right* Lamontagne/ The Garden Picture Library; *bottom left* David Cavagnaro **page 55:** *top left* David Cavagnaro; *top right* Jerry Pavia; *bottom right* Walter Chandoha; *bottom left* Neil Soderstrom **page 56:** *top* David Cavagnaro; *bottom left* Jerry Pavia; *bottom middle* David Cavagnaro; *bottom right* The Garden Picture Library **page 57:** *all* David Cavagnaro **page 58:** *all* David Cavagnaro **page 59** *all* David Cavagnaro **page 60:** *top* Lamontagne/The Garden Picture Library; *middle* The Garden Picture Library; *bottom* Derek Fell **page 61** *all* David Cavagnaro **page 62:** *top* David Cavagnaro; *middle* David Cavagnaro; *bottom* Positive Images **page 63:** *top left* David Cavagnaro; *top right* The Garden Picture Library; *bottom row* David Cavagnaro **page 64:** *top and middle* David Cavagnaro; *bottom row* Neil Soderstrom **page 65:** *top left* Charles Mann; *top right* David Cavagnaro; *bottom row* David Cavagnaro **page 66:** *top* David Cavagnaro; *bottom* The Garden Picture Library; *bottom right* Charles Mann **page 67:** *all* David Cavagnaro **page 68:** *all* David Cavagnaro **page 69:** *top and middle* David Cavagnaro; *bottom* Positive Images/Ben Phillips **page 70:** *top* David Cavagnaro; *middle* Neil Soderstrom; *bottom* David Cavagnaro **page 71:** *all* David Cavagnaro **page 72:** *top and bottom left* David Cavagnaro; *bottom right* Rob Cardillo **page 73:** *top* David Cavagnaro; *bottom* Positive Images/ Pam Spaulding **page 74:** *top* John Glover; *bottom left* and *right* David Cavagnaro **page 75:** *top left* and *middle* Neil Soderstrom; *top right* Photo Researchers/ Holt Studios/ Bob Gibbons; *bottom right* David Cavagnaro; *bottom left* Derek Fell **page 76:** *top* David Cavagnaro; *middle right* Derek Fell; *bottom left* David Cavagnaro **page 77:** *all* David Cavagnaro **page 78:** *top* Jerry Pavia; *bottom row* David Cavagnaro **page 79:** *top* Neil Soderstrom; *bottom left* David Cavagnaro; *bottom right* Karen Bussolini **page 80:** *all* David Cavagnaro **page 81:** *all* David Cavagnaro **page 82:** *top left* John Glover; *top right* David Cavagnaro; *bottom left* and *right* David Cavagnaro **page 83:** *top and bottom left* David Cavagnaro; *bottom right* Derek Fell **page 84:** *top* David Cavagnaro; *bottom* Neil Soderstrom **page 85:** *all* David Cavagnaro **page 86:** *top* Jerry Pavia; *bottom* Neil Soderstrom **page 87:** *all* David Cavagnaro **page 88:** *all* David Cavagnaro **page 89:** *top* and *bottom left* David Cavagnaro; *bottom right* Neil Soderstrom **page 90** *top right* and *bottom left* Neil Soderstrom; *bottom right* David Cavagnaro **page 91:** *top left* David Cavagnaro; *top right* Positive Images/Pam Spaulding; *bottom right* and *left* David Cavagnaro **page 96:** Catriona Tudor Erler

All illustrations by Mavis Torke.